THE VODKA 1000

The Ultimate Collection of Vodka Cocktails, Recipes, Facts, and Resources

Ray Foley

SOURCEBOOKS, INC.
NAPERVILLE, ILLINOIS

Published by Sourcebooks, Inc.
P.O. Box 4410, Naperville, Illinois 60567-4410
(630) 961-3900
Fax: (630) 961-2168
www.sourcebooks.com

Library of Congress Cataloging-in-Publication Data

Foley, Ray.
  Vodka 1000 : the ultimate collection of vodka cocktails, recipes, facts, and resources / Ray Foley.
      p. cm.
  Includes bibliographical references and index.
  ISBN 978-1-4022-1056-3 (trade pbk.)
  1. Cocktails. 2. Vodka. I. Title. II. Title: Vodka one thousand.

TX951.F596 2007
641.8'74--dc22
                              2007037533

Printed and bound in the United States of America.
          BG 10 9 8 7 6 5 4 3 2 1

DEDICATION

To Jaclyn Marie and Ryan Foley, and to the other tribe, Raymond, William, and Amy

To all the great readers of *Bartender Magazine* and www.bartender.com

CONTENTS

ACKNOWLEDGMENTS

We would like to thank the following individuals for their assistance in the completion of this book:

Olga Haley

AnnaMarie Battiloro, Associate Brand Manager, Absolut vodka

Julia Hall, Director of Media Services, Brown-Forman Corporation

Marguerite Provandie, Associate Director of Marketing services, White Rock Distilleries

Chet Zeigler, Admiral Wine

Chester Brandes and family, for answering all my questions about vodka . . . and for a great leg of lamb

Stephanie Carroll, for being awesome . . . and for dealing with me calling her "Pocahontas"

Erin Mackey, for her assistance . . . and for continuing her education

Loretta Natiello, for being my best friend

Jimmy Zazzalli, for being a great bartender and great friend

Matt Wojciak, John Cowan, Mike Cammarano, Charles Chop, Marvin Solomon, and of course the great Peter Lynch and Sara Kase, for all their assistance

Also, to all those who submitted recipes to www.Bartender.com and the readers of *Bartender Magazine*.

To all the great bartenders in America who have served me—you are the best!

INTRODUCTION

Welcome to the world of vodka. *Vodka 1000* gives you all the information you need to know about vodka—its history, cocktail recipes, food recipes, and even 100-plus websites about vodka.

Vodka is the most called-for ingredient in cocktails. There are over 150 different varieties on the market. We're sure you'll find ideas on how to use your personal favorite.

Both the home bartender and the professional bartender will find *Vodka 1000* to be a great reference.

A few notes on the recipes:

Sugar-free juice or diet pop can be substituted in any drink. For example, if a recipe calls for lemonade, feel free to use sugar-free lemonade; if a recipe calls for tonic, feel free to use diet tonic.

For martinis containing vermouth, the less vermouth, the drier the martini.

Enjoy, but please drink in moderation.

For more information on bartending, visit: www.bartender.com.

Chapter 1

50
VODKA FACTS

"Vodka" derives from the word "voda"

Vodka means "little water"

Vodka has been produced for over 650 years

Vodka was first distilled in Slavic countries

Vodka is now made in almost every country in the world

Vodka was originally made from potatoes

Now most vodka is made from grains
- Wheat
- Rye
- Beets
- Even hot peppers

A characteristic of vodka is that it has no distinctive color
- No aroma
- No taste

U.S. standards are that vodka must be a pure spirit
   No additives
   Except water

Most vodka is distilled at least three times
   Some is distilled four times
   Some is distilled five times
   Some is distilled six or more times

Many are filtered
   Some with charcoal
   Some with patented charcoal (Smirnoff)
   Others with glacia sand
   Quartz crystals
   Lava rock
   Champagne limestone
   Even Atlantic Irish Oak charcoal

Some vodkas use only pure rock mountain water
   Some use only heavy water (for every 6,000 lbs. of water there is
      only one part that contains heavy water)
   Iceberg water
   Irish spring water

Vodka comes in 100 proof
   94 proof
   90 proof
   86 proof
   80 proof

There are 124 calories in 1½ oz. of 100 proof vodka
   116 calories in 1½ oz. of 94 proof vodka
   110 calories in 1½ oz. of 90 proof vodka
   105 calories in 1½ oz. of 86 proof vodka
   97 calories in 1½ oz. of 80 proof vodka

There are 0 mg carbohydrates in vodka

There is 0 mg sodium in vodka

There is 0 g sugar in vodka

Using a q-tip, apply vodka to a cold sore to help dry it out

Using a cotton ball, apply vodka to cleanse the skin and tighten pores

To cure foot odor, wash your feet with vodka

Swish a shot of vodka over an aching tooth

750
VODKA RECIPES

3-SHEET MARTINI

1 oz. Three Olives Cherry vodka
1 oz. Three Olives raspberry vodka
½ oz. blue curacao
½ oz. strawberry liqueur
Splash of cranberry juice

Shake and serve.

'57 CHEVY

2 oz. Skyy vodka
1 oz. pineapple juice
1 oz. Grand Marnier
1 oz. Southern Comfort

Shake and serve.

A-BOMB

½ oz. vodka
½ oz. coffee liqueur
½ oz. Irish cream
½ oz. orange liqueur

Shake with ice and strain into a 7 oz. rocks glass.

ABSOLUT APPEAL

2 oz. Absolut Citron vodka
Lemonade
Club soda

Pour vodka over ice in a tall glass. Fill most of the way with lemonade. Top with a splash of club soda. Garnish with a lemon wedge.

ABSOLUT BRAVO

1 oz. Absolut vodka
½ oz. Campari
Tonic

Pour vodka and Campari over ice in a tall glass. Top with tonic. Garnish with a lemon slice and a lime slice.

ABSOLUT CITRON BREEZE

1¼ oz. Absolut Citron vodka
5 oz. grapefruit juice
3 oz. cranberry juice

Mix in a chilled glass with ice cubes. Garnish with a lime slice.

ABSOLUT CITRON COLLINS

1¼ oz. Absolut Citron vodka
1 oz. lemon juice
½ oz. sugar syrup
Club soda

Mix ingredients in a Collins glass. Stir well, add ice, garnish with fruit. Top with club soda.

ABSOLUT CITRON GODMOTHER

1¼ oz. Absolut Citron vodka
¾ oz. Hiram Walker Amaretto

Serve in a rocks glass over ice.

ABSOLUT CITRON RICKEY

2 oz. Absolut Citron vodka
Club soda

Pour Absolut Citron in a tall glass and fill with club soda. Add a squeeze of fresh lime.

ABSOLUT CITRON SOUR

2 oz. Absolut Citron vodka
¼ oz. lemon juice
1 tsp. sugar syrup

Mix in a shaker. Strain into a chilled glass and garnish with a cherry.

ABSOLUTION

1 part Absolut vodka
5 parts Mumm champagne

In a fluted champagne glass, mix the vodka and champagne. Cut a lemon peel in the form of a ring to represent a halo. The lemon peel can be either wrapped around the top of the glass or float on top of the champagne. (Thank you, Mr. James Caulfield.)

ABSOLUT LEMONADE

1¼ oz. Absolut Citron vodka
¼ oz. Hiram Walker triple sec
Sweet & sour mix
7 Up

Pour first two ingredients in a tall glass with ice and fill with ½ sweet & sour and ½ 7 Up. Mix, do not shake. Garnish with a lemon wheel.

ABSOLUT MONTAUK CITRON BREEZE

2 oz. Absolut Citron vodka
2 oz. grapefruit juice
2 oz. cranberry juice

Mix in a chilled Collins glass with ice cubes. Garnish with a lime slice.

ABSOLUT SQUEEZE

2 oz. Absolut Citron vodka
2 oz. orange juice
3 oz. pineapple juice
Splash Chambord

Pour vodka, orange juice, and pineapple juice in a tall glass over ice. Top with Chambord. Garnish with a lemon wedge, or try a whole strawberry.

ABSOLUT WHITE RUSSIAN

1 oz. Absolut vodka
½ oz. Godiva liqueur
Heavy cream

Shake and serve over ice in a rocks glass.

ADIOS

½ oz. Skyy vodka
½ oz. gin
½ oz. rum
½ oz. blue curacao
2 oz. sweet & sour mix
Splash of lemon-lime soda

Build over ice and fill with lemon-lime soda.

ADIOS MOTHER

½ oz. vodka
½ oz. blue curacao
½ oz. gin
½ oz. rum
2 oz. sweet & sour mix
Soda water

Build over ice in 12 oz. snifter and fill with soda water.

AFFAIR

1¼ oz. Absolut Kurant vodka
Cranberry juice
Club soda

Pour vodka over ice in a tall glass. Fill most of the way with cranberry juice and top with a splash of soda. Garnish with a wedge of lime.

AFTERBURNER

1 oz. peppered vodka
1 oz. cinnamon schnapps
1 oz. coffee liqueur

Shake with ice and strain into a shot glass.

AGENT O.

1½ oz. vodka
½ oz. orange liqueur
Orange juice

Pour first two ingredients into a glass over ice. Fill with orange juice. Shake. Garnish with an orange.

AIR GUNNER

2 oz. Sobieski vodka
Dash of blue curacao
1 oz. sour mix

Shake and strain into a chilled glass over ice.

ALABAMA SLAMMER

¾ oz. vodka
¾ oz. Southern Comfort
¾ oz. Amaretto
Dash of sloe gin or grenadine
Orange juice

Pour first four ingredients into a glass filled with ice. Fill with orange juice. Shake. Garnish with an orange slice.

ALASKAN ICED TEA

½ oz. vodka
½ oz. gin
½ oz. rum
1 oz. blue curacao
2 oz. sour mix
Lemon-lime soda.

Pour first five ingredients into a glass over ice. Fill with lemon-lime soda. Garnish with a lemon.

ALEXANDER THE GREAT

2 oz. Sobieski vodka
½ oz. Kahlua
½ oz. white crème de cacao
1 oz. double cream

Shake all ingredients with ice and strain into a chilled martini glass. Garnish with a few coffee beans.

ALICE-BE-BANANALESS

¾ oz. vodka
¾ oz. Amaretto
¾ oz. Midori
1 oz. cream

Shake with ice and strain into a 7 oz. rocks glass with ice.

ALLMONADE

2 oz. Absolut Citron vodka
1 oz. Amaretto
4 oz. lemonade
Lemon wedge

Stir and strain into a chilled sling glass.

AMBER MARTINI

2 oz. vanilla vodka
½ oz. Amaretto
½ oz. hazelnut liqueur

Stir with ice and strain into a chilled glass.

ANA'S BANANA

2 oz. vodka
½ fresh ripe banana
1 tsp. honey
Dash lime juice

Blend until smooth. Garnish with a banana.

AN ANGEL'S KISS

2 oz. Three Olives Cherry vodka

Stir in a cocktail glass over ice and garnish with a cherry.

ANTI-FREEZE

2 oz. vodka
½ oz. Midori

Shake with ice and strain into a glass.

APPLE BLOSSOM

3 oz. apple juice
1 oz. Yazi vodka
½ oz. amaretto

APPLE CIDER MARTINI

1 part Vox green apple vodka
1 part apple juice
Splash DeKuyper Hot Damn! cinnamon schnapps
Splash DeKuyper Buttershots schnapps

Shake with ice and strain into a martini glass.

APPLE ISLAND ICED TEA

1¼ parts Vox green apple vodka
¾ part Dekuyper Pucker sour apple schnapps
3 parts sweet & sour mix
1 part white soda

Build the first three ingredients over ice in a tall, green, sugar-rimmed glass. Top with white soda.

APPLE JOLL-E RANCHER

1½ oz. vodka
½ oz. sour apple schnapps
2 oz. sour mix

Shake with ice and fill with lemon lime soda.

APPLETINI

2 oz. Skyy vodka
1 oz. sour apple liqueur
Splash of lemon-lime soda

APRICOT COCKTAIL

1 oz. Skyy vodka
1 oz. apricot brandy
1 tbsp. fresh lemon juice
1 tbsp. fresh orange juice

AQUEDUCT

¾ oz. vodka
¼ oz. Hiram Walker Triple Sec
¼ oz. Hiram Walker Brandy
½ tbsp. lime juice

Shake with ice and strain into chilled cocktail glass.

ASIAN MARTINI

2½ oz. vodka
½ oz. ginger liqueur

Stir with ice and strain into a chilled martini glass.

ATOMIC BODY SLAM

½ oz. vodka
½ oz. gin
½ oz. dark rum
½ oz. blackberry brandy
Orange juice or grapefruit juice

Pour ingredients into a glass with ice and fill with orange juice or grape-fruit juice. Shake.

ATOMIC WASTE

¾ oz. vodka
¾ oz. melon liqueur
½ oz. peach schnapps
½ oz. banana liqueur
Milk

Pour first four ingredients into a glass with ice. Fill with milk. Shake. Strain into a chilled glass.

BABY DADDY

1 oz. Absolut vodka
1 oz. rum
½ oz. brandy
½ oz. butterscotch schnapps

Garnish with a maraschino cherry.

BABY FACE

¾ oz. vodka
¾ oz. crème de cassis
¾ oz. light cream

Shake all ingredients together firmly, with ice, in the shaker and strain into a glass.

BAILEY'S COMET

1½ oz. vodka
½ oz. Irish cream

Pour into a glass with ice.

BALALAIKA

1½ oz. Sobieski vodka
½ oz. Cointreau
2 oz. sour mix

Shake with ice and strain into a chilled glass. Garnish with a lime.

BALBOA CAFÉ MARTINI

1½ oz. Skyy vodka
Juice of half a fresh lemon
½ oz. bitters
Splash of grenadine
Splash of fresh orange juice

BALTIMORE ZOO

½ oz. vodka
½ oz. gin
½ oz. rum
½ oz. triple sec
1 oz. sour mix
Dash grenadine
Beer
Cola

Shake with ice. Fill with equal parts beer and cola. Garnish with a cherry, lime, lemon, and orange.

BAMBINI ARUBA

1 oz. vodka
½ oz. rum
½ oz. bourbon
Dash of grenadine
Sour mix
Orange juice
Pineapple juice

Pour first four ingredients into a glass with ice and fill with equal parts sour mix and orange and pineapple juice. Shake. Garnish with an orange or cherry.

BANANA BOAT FROZEN/TROPICAL

1½ oz. Three Olives vodka
1 oz. lime juice
½ peeled banana
1 tsp. honey

Blend with ice until smooth. Garnish with a lime wedge.

BANANA BOOMER

2½ oz. vodka
½ oz. DeKuyper crème de banana

Shake. Serve straight up or on the rocks.

BANANA CREAM

1 oz. Skyy vanilla vodka
1 oz. banana liqueur
½ oz. Frangelico
Splash of cream

Shake with ice. Serve straight up or on the rocks.

BANANA CREAM PIE

1 oz. vodka
½ oz. Irish cream
½ oz. banana liqueur
½ peeled ripe banana
Scoop of vanilla ice cream

Blend until smooth.

BANANA CREAM PIE MARTINI

2½ oz. vodka
Dash banana liqueur
Dash Irish cream

Shake with ice and strain into chilled glass.

BANANA NUT BREAD

1 oz. vodka or banana vodka
½ oz. hazelnut liqueur
½ oz. banana liqueur
¼ cup chopped walnuts
½ peeled ripe banana
Scoop of vanilla ice cream

Blend until smooth.

BANANA POPSICLE

1 oz. vodka
1 oz. banana liqueur
½ scoop orange sherbet
½ scoop vanilla ice cream
½ peeled ripe banana

Blend until smooth.

BANANA SPLIT

1½ oz. vodka
½ oz. banana liqueur
½ oz. strawberry liqueur
½ oz. dark crème de cacao
milk

Pour first four ingredients into a glass with ice and fill with milk. Shake.

BARNEY

2 oz. Three Olives Grape vodka
½ oz. blue curacao
½ oz. grenadine
Splash of tonic water

Shake with ice and strain into a chilled martini glass. Garnish with an orange slice.

BERT SIMPSIN

½ oz. vodka
½ oz. coconut rum
½ oz. melon liqueur

Shake with ice. Strain into a chilled glass.

BAY BREEZE

2 oz. Skyy vodka
1 oz. cranberry juice
1 oz. pineapple juice

BAY BREEZE TROPICAL

1½ oz. Three Olives vodka
4 oz. pineapple juice
1 oz. cranberry juice

Shake with ice and stir well. Garnish with a pineapple slice.

B.C.

1 part Absolut Citron vodka
1 part Godiva

Stir on the rocks.

BEACH BALL COOLER

1¼ oz. Absolut Citron vodka
½ oz. Hiram Walker Crème de Cassis
1 tsp. lime juice
Ginger ale

Mix in a Collins glass filled with ice. Fill with ginger ale. Garnish with a lemon and a cherry.

BEACH BUM

1 oz. Sobieski vodka
1½ oz. Midori
1 oz. cranberry juice

Shake with ice and strain into a cocktail glass. Serve straight up.

BELLA BELLA

1½ oz. Three Olives vodka
1 oz. Grand Marnier
1 oz. white cranberry juice
½ oz. lime juice

Shake with ice and strain into a chilled martini glass. Garnish with a cranberry.

BELLAGIO

2 oz. Skyy vodka
½ oz. passion fruit liqueur
½ oz. Campari
Splash of sugar syrup
Dash of fresh lemon juice

BERLIN WALL

1½ oz. vodka
½ Irish cream

Pour into a glass over ice and stir.

BERRYLICIOUS
(SERVED AS A LONG DRINK)

2 oz. vodka 02
¼ oz. Chambord
½ oz. raspberry puree
Ocean Spray Cranberry Juice

Pour first three ingredients into a glass and top with Ocean Spray Cranberry Juice. Garnish with lime wedge.

BERRYTINI

2 oz. Skyy berry vodka
1 oz. cranberry juice
Splash of lemon-lime soda

BERRY AND CRANBERRY JUICE

2 oz. Skyy berry vodka
Cranberry juice

Pour vodka into a glass and fill with cranberry juice.

BERRY AND SODA

2 oz. Skyy berry vodka
Skyy Soda

Pour vodka into a glass and fill with Skyy Soda.

BERRY BOMB

1½ oz. Skyy berry vodka
Energy drink

Pour vodka into a glass and top with any energy drink.

BERRY BURST

2 oz. Skyy berry vodka
½ oz. peach schnapps
½ oz. cranberry juice

Shake with ice. Serve over ice.

BERRY COLLINS

2 oz. Skyy berry vodka
Sweet & sour mix
Soda water

Pour vodka into a glass and fill with equal parts sweet & sour mix and soda water.

BERRY COSMO

2 oz. Skyy berry vodka
1 oz. triple sec
Splash of red or white cranberry juice
Fresh lime juice

Shake with ice. Serve over ice.

BERRY CRANTINI

2 oz. Skyy berry vodka
1 oz. cranberry juice
½ oz. triple sec

Shake with ice. Serve over ice.

BERRY DROP

1 oz. Skyy berry vodka
1 oz. Skyy citrus vodka
Splash of sweet & sour mix
Splash of fresh lemon juice

Shake with ice. Serve over ice.

BERRY LEMONADE

2 oz. vodka
¼ oz. strawberry liqueur

Pour over ice in a tall glass. Garnish with a fresh strawberry.

BERRY METROPOLITAN

2 oz. Skyy berry vodka
1 oz. raspberry liqueur
Splash of lemon-lime soda

BERRY SEA BREEZE

2 oz. Skyy berry vodka
Cranberry juice
Pineapple juice

Pour vodka in a glass and fill with equal parts cranberry juice and pineapple juice.

BERRY WHITE

1 oz. UV Blue vodka
1 oz. crème de cacao
1½ oz. triple sec
1 part lime juice

Shake with ice and strain into a martini glass.

BIG DADDY

½ oz. vodka or citrus vodka
½ oz. rum
½ oz. tequila
½ oz. whiskey
Lemon-lime soda

Pour first four ingredients into a glass over ice and fill with lemon-lime soda. Garnish with a lime.

BIKINI

1 oz. vodka
1 oz. rum
1 tsp. sugar
1 oz. sour mix
1 oz. cream or milk

Shake with ice and strain into a chilled glass.

BIKINI LINE

¾ oz. vodka
¾ oz. raspberry liqueur
¾ oz. coffee liqueur

Pour into a glass over ice.

BIKINI MARTINI

2 oz. Skyy vodka
½ oz. coconut rum
Splash of orange juice
Splash of pineapple juice

BIMINI ICE-T

½ oz. vodka
½ oz. gin
½ oz. spiced rum
½ oz. tequila
½ oz. blue curacao
1 oz. sour mix
1 oz. orange juice
1 oz. pineapple juice
Cola

Shake first eight ingredients in a glass over ice. Top with cola. Garnish with a lemon.

BITTER CITRUS

2 oz. Skyy citrus vodka
½ tsp. superfine sugar
4 oz. tonic water

BLACK

½ oz. Skyy vodka
½ oz. coffee liqueur
½ oz. cream

BLACK CAT

1 oz. Sobieski vodka
1 oz. cherry liqueur
Cranberry juice
Cola

Pour first two ingredients into a glass with ice. Fill with equal parts cranberry juice and cola.

BLACK COW

1 oz. Sobieski vodka
1 oz. dark crème de cacao
Cream or milk

Pour first two ingredients into a glass over ice and fill with cream or milk. Shake.

BLACK DRAGON

½ oz. Kremlyovskaya chocolate vodka
½ oz. cherry brandy
½ oz. Bacardi 151

Layer in a shot glass.

BLACK EYE

1½ oz. vodka
½ oz. Hiram Walker blackberry brandy

Stir. Serve up or on the rocks.

BLACK FOREST

In blender:
½ cup ice
¾ oz. vodka
¾ oz. coffee liqueur
¾ oz. black raspberry liqueur
Scoop of chocolate ice cream

Blend until smooth. Garnish with sprinkles.

BLACK MAGIC

1½ oz. vodka
¾ oz. coffee liqueur

Mix with cracked ice in a shaker or blender and pour into a chilled old-fashioned glass. Add several dashes of lemon juice.

BLACK ORCHID

1 oz. Sobieski vodka
½ oz. blue curacao
1½ oz. cranberry juice

Build over ice in a 7 oz. rocks glass.

BLACK CHERRY VODKA AND COLA

1½ oz. Smirnoff Black Cherry vodka
3 oz. cola

Build over ice. Stir well.

BLACK RUSSIAN

1½ oz. Smirnoff vodka
¾ oz. Kahlua

Build over cubed ice and stir briskly. Garnish with swizzle stick.

BLACK RUSSIAN CLASSIC

2 oz. Three Olives vodka
1 oz. coffee liqueur
Splash lemon juice

Build over ice and stir well.

BLACKBERRY SIP

2 oz. Skyy vodka
1 oz. blackberry brandy
1 oz. sweet & sour mix

BLEACHER CREATURE

⅓ oz. vodka
⅓ oz. tequila
⅓ oz. rum
⅓ oz. triple sec
⅓ oz. melon liqueur
⅓ oz. green crème de menthe
Sour mix

Pour first six ingredients into a glass over ice and fill with sour mix. Shake.

BLESSED KISS

2 oz. Three Olives Grape vodka
1 oz. Three Olives Vanilla vodka
Splash of cranberry juice

Shake with ice and strain into a chilled martini glass. Garnish with a lime wedge.

BLIND MELON

1 oz. melon liqueur
½ oz vodka or orange vodka
½ oz. rum
½ oz. triple sec

Shake with ice and strain into a chilled glass.

BLING OUT

2 parts Absolut vodka
2 parts lemon juice
1 part saffron sugar syrup
4 dashes of Cointreau
2 dashes of orange juice

Shake with ice and strain into a chilled cocktail glass.
How to make saffron sugar syrup (3dl): Heat 3dl of water and 3dl of sugar with 0.5g of saffron. Stir until the sugar has completely dissolved. Let syrup cool before using it in the cocktail.

BLIZZARD

1¼ oz. Sobieski vodka
Fresca

Pour vodka into a tall glass over ice and fill with Fresca. Garnish with a twist of lemon.

BLOOD ORANGE

2 oz. Skyy vodka
1 oz. Campari
Orange juice

Build in a glass and fill with orange juice. Garnish with a slice of orange.

BLOOD ORANGE MARTINI

3½ oz. vodka
Dash orange liqueur
Dash Campari
Dash blood orange juice or orange juice

Shake with ice and strain into a chilled martini glass.

BLOODY BREW

1½ oz. vodka
2 oz. tomato juice
Beer or malt liquor

*Pour first two ingredients into a glass and fill with beer or malt liquor.
Garnish with a dash of salt.*

BLOODY BULL

2 oz. vodka
1 oz. beef bouillon
1 tsp. horseradish
3 dashes Tabasco sauce
3 dashes Worcestershire sauce
Dash lime juice
3 dashes celery salt
3 dashes pepper
1 oz. clam juice (optional)
Dash of sherry (optional)
Tomato juice

*Pour first 10 ingredients into a glass over ice and fill with tomato juice.
Pour from one glass to another until mixed. Garnish with lemon or lime
wedge.*

BLOODY CAESAR

1¼ oz. Sobieski vodka
3 oz. Clamato juice

Build over ice. Add dash of Tabasco, Worcestershire, pepper, and salt. Garnish with celery stalk or lime wheel.

BLOODY DELICIOUS

2 parts UV vodka
2 parts tomato juice
1 part celery salt
1 part Tabasco sauce
1 part Worcestershire sauce

Serve over ice in a highball glass.

BLOODY MARIA

2 oz. Skyy vodka
4 oz. tomato juice
1½ tsp. fresh lime juice
1 tsp. dry sherry
¼ tsp. Frank's Redhot Original Cayenne Pepper Sauce
¼ tsp. Worcestershire Sauce
¼ tsp. celery salt or seeds
Coarsely ground black pepper and salt to taste

BLOODY MARY ON A STICK

1½ oz. Teton Glacier potato vodka
Think of vermouth

Shake with ice and strain into a martini glass. Garnish with a cherry tomato.

BLUE 7

2 oz. vodka 02
⅛ oz. blue curacao
Apple juice

Shake all ingredients and serve on ice in a 14 oz. glass. Top with good-quality, sweet apple juice. Garnish with an orange slice or twist.

BLUE BOMBSICLE

1 part UV Blue vodka
3 parts lemonade

Serve over ice in a lowball glass.

BLUE BALL MARTINI

2 oz. Three Olives Grape vodka
1 oz. blue curacao
1 oz. peach schnapps

Shake with ice and strain into a chilled martini glass. Garnish with an orange slice.

BLUE BAYOU

1 oz. Skyy vodka
1 oz. blue curacao
Equal amounts of pineapple juice and grapefruit juice

BLUE BLOCKER

2 oz. Ohranj vodka
½ oz. blue curacao

Serve over ice.

BLUE BULLS COCKTAIL

1 oz. Three Olives vodka
1 oz. blue curacao
Energy drink

Build over ice in a cocktail glass and fill with any energy drink.

BLUE FROST

1 part UV Blue vodka
1 part raspberry sherbet
1 part lemon-lime soda

Serve over ice in a lowball glass.

BLUE HARVEST

2 oz. Skyy vodka
1 oz. blue curacao
1 oz. triple sec
Splash of lemon-lime soda

BLUE HAWAIIAN

1½ oz. vodka
½ oz. blue curacao
Orange juice
Pineapple juice

Pour first two ingredients into a glass over ice and fill with equal parts orange and pineapple juice. Shake. Garnish with pineapple.

BLUE HOUND

2 oz. Skyy vodka
1 oz. grapefruit juice

BLUE KAMIKAZE

2 oz. vodka
½ oz. blue curacao
Dash lime juice

Shake with ice. Garnish with a pineapple slice.

BLUE LAGOON TROPICAL

1½ oz. Three Olives vodka
½ oz. blue curacao
4 oz. pineapple juice

Build over ice and stir well. Garnish with a pineapple slice.

BLUE LEMONADE

1 oz. Skyy vodka
½ oz. blue curacao
Lemonade

Build over ice and fill with lemonade.

BLUE MEANIE

1½ oz. Sobieski vodka
½ oz. blue curacao
2 oz. sour mix

Shake with ice and strain into shot glass.

BLUE ORCHARD COSMOPOLITAN

2 parts Vox green apple vodka
2 parts cranberry juice
1 part DeKuyper Pucker Island blue schnapps

Shake with ice and strain into a martini glass.

BLUE SHARK

1 oz. vodka
1 oz. tequila
½ oz. blue curacao

Shake with ice and strain into a chilled glass.

BLUE SLEEPER FROZEN

¼ oz. Three Olives vodka
¼ oz. sour apple schnapps
¼ oz. triple sec
½ oz. blue curacao
¾ oz. Smirnoff Ice
¼ oz. sour mix

Blend with ice.

BLUE-UP

1 part Stoli Blueberi
Splash of blue curacao

Shake with ice and strain into a shot glass.

BLUSHING RUSSIAN

2 oz. Three Olives Grape vodka
1 oz. Three Olives chocolate vodka
1 oz. Irish cream
Splash of Kaluha

Shake with ice and strain into a chilled martini glass.

BOCCI BALL

1¼ oz. vodka
¾ oz. Hiram Walker Amaretto
1 oz. orange juice

Serve straight up or on the rocks.

BON BON

1 oz. Absolut Kurant vodka
½ oz. Godiva liqueur

Combine in a brandy snifter.

BOSTON GOLD

1½ oz. Absolut vodka
½ oz. banana liqueur
Orange juice

*Pour first two ingredients into a glass over ice and fill with orange juice.
Shake.*

BOSTON ICED TEA

½ oz. vodka
½ oz. gin
½ oz. rum
½ oz. coffee liqueur
½ oz. amaretto
2 oz. sour mix
Cola

Pour first six ingredients into a glass over ice and fill with cola. Garnish with a lemon wedge.

BOSTON TEA PARTY

1 oz. vodka
½ oz. amaretto
½ oz. coffee liqueur
½ oz. Cointreau
2 oz. sour mix
Cola

Shake first five ingredients with ice. Fill with cola.

BOUGHS OF HOLLY

1 oz. Skyy melon vodka
¼ oz. lime juice
Splash of sweet & sour mix
Splash of lemon-lime soda

BOUNTY MARTINI

1½ oz. vodka
1 oz. vanilla vodka
1½ oz. Coco Lopez
¼ oz. sugar syrup
4 dashes orange bitters
3 fresh strawberries

Muddle the strawberries with the vodka in the base of a shaker. Pour in the cream of coconut, sugar syrup, and the bitters, shake all ingredients with ice, and strain into a chilled martini glass. Garnish with a fresh strawberry.

BOXING SHORTS

2 parts Kremlyovskaya chocolate vodka
1 part peach schnapps

Shake with ice and strain into a shot glass.

BRAIN WAVE (FLOATER)

1¼ oz. Irish cream (bottom)
¾ oz. vodka (top)

Place a drop of grenadine into center of drink.

BRASS MONKEY

2 oz. Skyy vodka
2 oz. light rum
Orange juice

Pour first two ingredients into a glass and fill with orange juice.

BRAZILIAN ORANGETINI

2 oz. Skyy orange vodka
1 oz. fresh orange juice

BROKEN DOWN GOLF CART

1 oz. vodka
1 oz. amaretto
1 oz. cranberry juice

Shake with ice and strain into shot glass.

BROKEN HEART

1 oz. vodka
1 oz. black raspberry liqueur
Dash of grenadine
Orange juice

Pour first three ingredients into a glass over ice and shake. Fill with orange juice.

BROWN BEAR

1 oz. vodka
1½ oz. coffee liqueur

Shake with ice and strain into a stemmed glass. Top with cola.

BROWN DERBY

¼ oz. Absolut vodka
3 oz. cola

Serve in a tall glass with ice.

BUBBLE GUM

1 oz. cranberry vodka
¼ oz. peach schnapps
¼ oz. crème de banana
1 oz. orange juice

Shake and serve over ice.

BUBBLE LOUNGE MARTINI

2 oz. Skyy vodka
1 oz. champagne
Splash of fresh tangerine juice

BULLFROG

1½ oz. Smirnoff vodka
5 oz. limeade

Combine in a tall glass over ice. Stir and garnish with a wedge of lime.

BURNT ALMOND

1 oz. vodka
1 oz. coffee liqueur
1 oz. amaretto
Milk or cream.

Shake with ice.

BURNT ALMOND (FROZEN)

In blender:
½ cup ice
1 oz. vodka
1 oz. coffee liqueur
½ oz. amaretto
Scoop of vanilla ice cream

Blend until smooth.

BURNTOUT BITCH

½ oz. vodka
½ oz. rum
½ oz. tequila
½ oz. triple sec
Orange juice

Pour first four ingredients into a glass over ice and fill with orange juice. Shake.

BUTTAFINGER

½ oz. vodka or vanilla vodka
1 oz. cookies and cream liqueur
1 oz. butterscotch schnapps
Cream or milk

Pour first three ingredients into a glass and fill with cream or milk. Shake with ice.

BUTTERSCOTCH BOMBER

½ oz. vodka
½ oz. Baileys Irish Cream
½ oz. DeKuyper Buttershots schnapps

Shake with ice.

CAJUN MARTINI

1¼ oz. Peppar vodka
Dash of extra-dry vermouth

Shake or stir well with ice and strain into a cocktail glass, or serve over ice. Garnish with a twist or an olive.

CAJUNTINI

2 oz. Skyy vodka
1 oz. triple sec
Splash of jalapeno juice
Splash of sweet & sour mix
Dash of Tabasco
Olives
Dash of black pepper

Garnish with a lemon slice.

CAKE SLICE

2 parts Absolut vodka
1 part Limoncello
2 parts fresh-pressed apple juice
Lemon slice
Pistachio nut, chopped

Shake with ice and strain into a chilled cocktail glass.

CALIFORNIA ICED TEA

½ oz. Sobieski vodka
½ oz. gin
½ oz. rum
½ oz. tequila
½ oz. triple sec
2 oz. grapefruit juice
Cola

Pour first six ingredients into a glass over ice and top with cola. Garnish with a lemon.

CALIFORNIA LEMONADE

1 oz. Smirnoff Red Label vodka
¼ oz. Tanqueray London Dry gin
¼ oz. cognac
¼ oz. grenadine
2 oz. orange juice
Splash lime juice
Splash sugar syrup

Shake and serve over ice in a hurricane glass. Garnish with a lemon wedge.

CAMPARI COSMO

2 oz. Skyy citrus vodka
1 oz. Campari
1 oz. orange juice
Splash of triple sec

CANDY CANE

¾ oz. Skyy berry vodka
¾ oz. peppermint schnapps
¾ oz. white crème de cacao
¼ oz. grenadine
Half-and-half
Soda water

CAPE CODDER

1½ oz. Sobieski vodka
4 oz. cranberry juice
Club soda

Build first two ingredients over cubed ice in Collins glass. Fill with club soda and stir well. Garnish with orange slices on right side of glass and two 9-inch straws.

CAPP

2 oz. Skyy orange vodka
1 oz. apple liqueur
2 oz. cranberry juice (or white cranberry juice)

CAPPUCHENKO

½ oz. Stolichnaya Zinamon vodka
1 oz. Stolichnaya Kafya vodka
½ oz. Stolichnaya Vanil vodka

Pour all ingredients over ice in a large mixing glass or cocktail shaker. Stir and strain into a chilled martini glass.

CARAMEL APPLE MARTINI

1 oz. Three Olives green apple vodka
½ oz. apple schnapps
1 oz. butterscotch liqueur
2 oz. half-and-half

Shake with ice and strain into a martini glass drizzled with caramel sauce. Garnish with Granny Smith apple.

CARAMEL APPLETINI

2 parts UV apple vodka
1 part butterscotch schnapps

Shake with ice and strain into a martini glass.

CARMEN MIRANDA

2 oz. Three Olives vodka
½ oz. coconut rum
½ oz. triple sec
2 drops orange bitters

Shake with ice and strain into a chilled martini glass. Garnish with a lime wedge.

CARIBBEAN BREEZE

2 oz. Skyy vodka
1 oz. coconut rum
2 dashes of grenadine
Orange juice

Build first three ingredients and fill with orange juice.

CAT SCRATCH FEVER SHOT

½ oz. Three Olives vodka
¼ oz. Southern Comfort
¼ oz. amaretto
½ oz. pineapple juice

Shake with ice and strain into a shot glass.

CELTIC COMRADE (FLOATER)

½ oz. coffee liqueur (bottom)
½ oz. Irish cream
½ oz. vodka
½ oz. Drambuie (top)

CENTRAL PARK MARTINI

3 oz. Teton Glacier potato vodka
2 tbsp. pineapple juice
1 tbsp. Chambord

Shake with ice. Serve in a chilled martini glass with a sprig of parsley as a garnish.

CHAI'NA DOLL

8 oz. iced chai with milk
1 oz. Yazi

CHAMPAGNE LADY

1 oz. Vox raspberry vodka
½ oz. Chambord
½ oz. sour mix
½ oz. cranberry juice
Float of champagne

Rim a martini glass with sugar; set aside. In a mixing glass, combine vodka, Chambord, sour mix, and cranberry juice. Strain into martini glass and float champagne.

CHAMPAGNE SUPERNOVA

½ oz. vodka
½ oz. gin
½ oz. blue curacao
Dash of cranberry juice
Dash of sour mix
Champagne

Pour first five ingredients into a glass with ice and fill with champagne.

CHAMP-TINI

1½ oz. Ciroc vodka
Splash of honey liqueur
Moet & Chandon Nectar Imperial

Pour first two ingredients into a glass and top with Moet & Chandon Nectar Imperial. Garnish with a lemon peel.

CHARD-TINI

¾ oz. Cîroc vodka
¾ oz. Sterling Vineyards Chardonnay
¼ oz. peach schnapps
1 oz. lemon-lime soda

Shake vodka, chardonnay, and schnapps with ice. Strain and top with lemon-lime soda.

CHEAP SHADES

1 oz. vodka or pineapple vodka
½ oz. peach schnapps
½ oz. melon liqueur
Dash sour mix
Dash pineapple juice
Lemon-lime soda

Pour first five ingredients into a glass over ice and fill with lemon-lime soda. Garnish with pineapple slice.

CHEAP SUNGLASSES

2 oz. vodka
Cranberry juice
Lemon-lime soda

*Pour vodka into a glass over ice and fill with equal parts cranberry juice
and lemon-lime soda. Garnish with pineapple slice.*

CHEESECAKE MARTINI

¾ oz. Smirnoff strawberry vodka
¾ oz. Smirnoff Vanilla vodka
Splash cranberry juice

Shake with ice and strain into a martini glass.

CHERRY BOMB

1 part UV Cherry vodka
3 parts cola or energy drink

Serve over ice in a lowball glass.

CHERRY BOOTS

1 oz. Three Olives cherry vodka
1 oz. Three Olives vanilla vodka
1 oz. Kahlua
½ oz. sour mix
½ oz. grenadine

Shake with ice and strain into a chilled martini glass. Garnish with a cherry.

CHERRY COBBLER

1½ oz. Skyy berry vodka
½ oz. amaretto
¼ oz. crème de cocoa
½ oz. sour mix
Splash of cranberry juice

CHERRY COLA

2 oz. Three Olives Cherry vodka
3 oz. cola

Mix in a highball glass with ice. Garnish with a cherry.

CHERRY CHEESECAKE

1 oz. Three Olives Cherry vodka
1 oz. Three Olives Vanilla vodka
1 oz. cranberry juice

Shake with ice and strain into a chilled martini glass. Garnish with a cherry.

CHERRY CORDIAL

1 oz. Three Olives Cherry vodka
1 oz. Three Olives chocolate vodka
¼ oz. white crème de cacao
Splash of grenadine

Shake with ice and strain into a chocolate rimmed martini glass. Garnish with a cherry.

CHERRY COSMO

1 part UV Cherry vodka
1 part triple sec
1 part cranberry juice

Shake with ice and strain into a martini glass.

CHERRY DAIQUIRI

1 oz. Three Olives Cherry vodka
1 oz. lime juice
1 oz. cherry brandy
1 tsp. sugar

Pour ingredients into a blender with two cups of crushed ice. Blend at high speed and pour into a hurricane glass. Garnish with a cherry.

CHERRY DROP

1 oz. Three Olives Cherry vodka
½ oz. triple sec
Splash of lemon-lime soda
Splash of sour mix

Mix ingredients and pour into a chilled, sugar-rimmed martini glass filled with dry ice. Result is a smoky, bubbly effect.

CHERRY KAMIKAZE MARTINI

1 oz. Three Olives Cherry vodka
½ oz. triple sec
2 oz. sour mix

Shake with ice and strain into a chilled martini glass. Garnish with a cherry.

CHERRY MARTINI

2½ oz. Three Olives Cherry vodka
Splash of lime juice

Shake with ice and strain into a chilled martini glass. Garnish with a cherry and a lime wedge.

CHERRY PIE

1 oz. vodka
½ oz. brandy
½ oz. cherry brandy

Stir with ice and strain into a chilled glass.

CHERRY SQUIRT

2 oz. Three Olives Cherry vodka
2 oz. lemonade
½ oz. triple sec

Shake with ice and strain into a chilled martini glass. Garnish with a cherry.

CHERRY VODKA TONIC

2 oz. Three Olives Cherry vodka
4 oz. tonic

Mix in a highball glass with ice. Garnish with a lime wedge.

CHI CHI

1½ oz. Absolut vodka
¾ oz. pineapple juice
1½ oz. Cream of coconut

Blend with ice to slush. Garnish with a cherry.

CHICKEN SHOT

2 oz. vodka
1 oz. chicken bouillon
Dash Worcestershire sauce
Dash of salt
Dash of pepper

CHINA BEACH

1 oz. vodka
1 oz. ginger liqueur
Cranberry juice

Pour first two ingredients into a glass over ice and fill with cranberry juice. Stir.

CHINA C

2 oz. tangerine liquor
1 oz. Yazi
4 oz. seltzer water

CHOCOLATE BASH

1 oz. Kremlyovskaya
½ oz. Chambord
¼ oz. cream
⅛ oz. club soda

Pour first three ingredients into a glass and top with soda.

CHOCOLATE CAKE

¾ oz. citrus vodka
¾ oz. hazelnut liqueur

Stir with ice and strain into a shot glass. Garnish with a sugarcoated lemon.

CHOCOLATE CHAOS (FROZEN)

1½ oz. chocolate vodka
½ oz. crème de cacao
2 oz. chocolate syrup
Scoop of chocolate ice cream

Blend until smooth. Top with chocolate whipped cream. Garnish with a chocolate graham cracker.

CHOCOLATE CHERRY JUBILEE

1 oz. Three Olives cherry vodka
1 oz. Three Olives chocolate vodka
1 oz. grenadine

Shake with ice and strain into a chilled martini glass. Drizzle chocolate syrup on top. Garnish with a cherry.

CHOCOLATE CHERRY SURPRISE

1 part Starbucks Coffee liqueur
½ part DeKuyper Razzmatazz liqueur
½ part Vox raspberry vodka
1 part cream

Shake over ice.

CHOCOLATE CHIP

2 oz. Skyy vodka, chilled
½ oz. Frangelico

CHOCOLATE-COVERED CHERRY

1 oz. Three Olives Cherry vodka
1 oz. White Crème de Cacao

CHOCOLATE COCONUT DREAM CREAM MARTINI

1 oz. half-and-half
1 oz. Van Gogh Chocolate liqueur
1 oz. Van Gogh Coconut vodka
1 oz. Van Gogh Dutch chocolate vodka

Pour ingredients into a cocktail shaker. Add crushed ice and let stand for five seconds. Shake vigorously for five seconds and strain into a double martini glass. Garnish with melon baller scoop of chocolate ice cream.

CHOCOLATE COVERED ORANGE

1 oz. Skyy orange vodka
2 oz. Vermeer Dutch Chocolate cream

CHOCOLATE-DIPPED BERRY

1 oz. Three Olives berry vodka
1 oz. Three Olives chocolate vodka
½ oz. white crème de cacao

Shake with ice and strain into a chocolate rimmed martini glass.

CHOCOLATE EGG CRÈME

1½ oz. Kremlyovskaya vodka
½ oz. Baileys Irish cream
7 Up

Build first three ingredients in a hurricane glass over crushed ice. Fill with 7 Up and top with chocolate syrup.

CHOCOLATE LATTE

2 parts Vox vodka
1 part DeKuyper crème de cacao
1 part cream

CHOCOLATE MARTINI

1¼ oz. Absolut Kurant vodka
Dash of white crème de cacao

Shake or stir well over ice and strain into a chocolate-rimmed cocktail glass, straight up or over ice. Garnish with an orange peel. (Hint: to rim the glass, first rub a piece of orange around the top of the glass, then gently place the glass upside down in a plate of unsweetened chocolate powder.)

CHOCOLATE ORANGE

1½ oz. Skyy orange vodka
½ oz. chocolate liqueur
½ oz. Grand Marnier

CHOCOLATE THUNDER

2 oz. Sobieski vodka
Chocolate milk

Pour vodka into a glass and fill with chocolate milk.

CIELO

2 oz. Skyy vodka
1 oz. crème de cassis
Splash of ginger ale
Juice of half a lime

CILVER CITRON

2 oz. Absolut Citron vodka
½ oz. Mumm champagne

Serve straight up.

CITRON AND SODA

2 oz. Absolut Citron vodka
Club soda

Pour vodka over ice in a tall glass. Fill with club soda. Garnish with a lemon twist.

CITRON CELEBRATION

2 oz. Absolut Citron vodka

Serve on the rocks.

CITRON CODDER

1½ oz. Absolut Citron vodka
Cranberry juice

Pour vodka into a glass and fill with cranberry juice. Serve in a tall glass with ice.

CITRON COOLER

1¼ oz. Absolut Citron vodka
½ oz. fresh lime juice
Tonic

Build first two ingredients over ice in a tall glass and fill with tonic. Garnish with a lime wedge.

CITRON KAMIKAZE

¾ oz. Absolut Citron vodka
¾ oz. triple sec
⅛ oz. lime juice

Shake well with ice and strain into a cocktail glass. Serve straight up or on the rocks. Garnish with a lime wedge.

CITRON MADRAS

2 oz. Absolut Citron vodka
Orange juice
Cranberry juice

In a tall glass with ice, fill with half orange juice and half cranberry juice.

CITRON MARTINI

2¼ oz. citron
Dash of extra-dry vermouth

Shake or stir well with ice and strain into a cocktail glass, straight up or over ice. Garnish with a twist or an olive.

CITRUS APPLETINI

2 oz. Skyy citrus vodka
½ oz. sour apple liqueur
Splash of lemon-lime soda

CITRUS AVIATOR

2 oz. Skyy citrus vodka
½ oz. maraschino cherry juice
½ oz. lemon juice

CITRUS BANSHEE

1 oz. Skyy citrus vodka
½ oz. banana liqueur
½ oz. white crème de cacao
Cream

Pour first three ingredients into a glass and top with cream.

CITRUS BELLINI

2 oz. Skyy citrus vodka
1 oz. peach schnapps
¼ oz. grenadine

CITRUS BLOOD ORANGE

2 oz. Skyy citrus vodka
1 oz. Campari
Orange juice

Pour first two ingredients into a glass and fill with orange juice. Garnish with a slice of orange.

CITRUS CALIFORNIA

2 oz. Skyy citrus vodka
Orange juice
Grapefruit juice

Pour vodka into a glass and fill with equal parts orange juice and grape-fruit juice.

CITRUS CHIQUITA

2 oz. Skyy citrus vodka
½ oz. banana liquor
1 tsp. Orgeat (almond) syrup

CITRUS CHOCOTINI

2 oz. Skyy citrus vodka
1 oz. Vermeer Chocolate Cream

CITRUS COLLINS

2 oz. Skyy citrus vodka
1 oz. lemon juice
Lemon-lime soda

Pour first two ingredients into a glass and fill with lemon-lime soda. Garnish with a cherry and an orange slice.

CITRUS COOLER

2 oz. Skyy citrus vodka
Lemon-lime soda

Pour vodka into a glass and fill with lemon-lime soda. Garnish with a lemon wedge.

CITRUS CRANTINI

2 oz. Skyy citrus vodka
½ oz. triple sec
Splash of cranberry juice

CITRUS COSMO

2 oz. Skyy citrus vodka
1 oz. triple sec
Splash of cranberry juice
Lots of fresh lime juice

CITRUS COSMOBLANCA

2 oz. Skyy citrus vodka
1 oz. white cranberry juice
Splash of triple sec
Fresh lime juice

CITRUS DROP

2 oz. Skyy citrus vodka
1 oz. triple sec
Squeeze of fresh lemon juice

CITRUS DROP MARTINI

2 oz. Skyy citrus vodka
¼ oz. triple sec
¼ oz. lemon juice
Sugar

CITRUS ELECTRIC LEMONADE

2 oz. Skyy citrus vodka
1 oz. blue curacao
Fresh lemonade

Pour first two ingredients into a glass and fill with fresh lemonade.

CITRUS FALLING STAR

1½ oz. Skyy citrus vodka
1½ oz. triple sec
½ tsp. super fine sugar

Garnish with a lemon wedge.

CITRUS FRENCH MARTINI

2 oz. Skyy citrus vodka
½ oz. raspberry liqueur
Splash of pineapple juice

CITRUS FUZZY MARTINI

2 oz. Skyy citrus vodka
½ oz. peach schnapps

CITRUS FUZZY NAVEL

2 oz. Skyy citrus vodka
1 oz. peach schnapps
Orange juice

Pour first two ingredients into a glass and fill with orange juice.

CITRUS GIMLET

2 oz. Skyy citrus vodka
⅛ oz. Fresh lime juice

CITRUS GLACIER MINT

2 oz. Skyy vodka
½ oz. Skyy citrus vodka
½ oz. green crème de menthe

CITRUS GOLDEN RULE

2 oz. Skyy citrus vodka
½ oz. Grand Marnier
Orange juice

Pour first two ingredients into a glass and fill with orange juice.

CITRUS ISLAND

2 oz. Skyy citrus vodka, chilled
½ oz. coconut rum, chilled
½ oz. Midori melon liqueur, chilled

CITRUS LEMONTINI

2 oz. Skyy citrus vodka
1 oz. sour mix
Splash of club soda

CITRUS MADRAS

2 oz. Skyy citrus vodka
Cranberry juice
Orange juice

Pour vodka into a glass and fill with equal parts cranberry juice and orange juice. Garnish with a lime wedge.

CITRUS MARGARITA

2 oz. Skyy citrus vodka
½ oz. triple sec
3 oz. sour mix
Splash of orange juice

CITRUS MARTINI

3 oz. Teton Glacier potato vodka
2 tbsp. fresh lime juice
1 tbsp. triple sec

CITRUS MELON BALL

2 oz. Skyy citrus vodka
1 oz. Midori melon liqueur
Orange juice

Pour first two ingredients into a glass and fill with orange juice.

CITRUS MOJITO

2 oz. Skyy citrus vodka
3 crushed fresh mint leaves
Spoonful of sugar
Splash of sweet & sour
4 oz. soda water
⅛ oz. fresh lime juice

CITRUS PEACHES AND CREAM

2 oz. Skyy citrus vodka
1 oz. peach liqueur
Splash of cream

CITRUS PETIT ZINC

2 oz. Skyy citrus vodka
½ oz. Cinzano sweet vermouth
½ oz. orange juice

CITRUS QUENCH

2 oz. Skyy citrus vodka
Fresh pomegranate juice
Splash of triple sec

CITRUS RASPBERRY LEMONADE

2 oz. Skyy citrus vodka
1 oz. raspberry liqueur
Fresh lemonade

Pour first two ingredients into a glass and fill with fresh lemonade.

CITRUS SCREAMING GRASSHOPPER

1½ oz. Skyy citrus vodka
½ oz. white crème de cacao
½ oz. white crème de menthe
Splash of heavy cream

CITRUS SPRITZER

1 part UV citrus vodka
3 parts lemon-lime soda

Serve over ice in a highball glass.

CITRUS STAR

2 oz. Skyy citrus vodka
1 oz. Midori melon liqueur
½ oz. triple sec
½ oz. sweet & sour mix
Lemonade

Pour first four ingredients into a glass and top with lemonade.

CITRUS SUNRISE

2 oz. Skyy citrus vodka
3½ oz. orange juice
¼ oz. grenadine

CITRUS SUNSET

1 part Vox vodka
1 part DeKuyper Pucker watermelon schnapps
½ part DeKuyper orange curacao
Splash of 7 Up

Shake and strain into a glass.

CITRUS SUNSET

1 oz. Smirnoff citrus vodka
½ oz. Captain Morgan Parrot Bay Coconut Rum
2 oz. cranberry juice
2 oz. pineapple juice

Build over ice and stir well. Garnish with a lime wedge.

CITRUS TART

2 oz. Skyy citrus vodka
1 oz. grapefruit juice
1 oz. raspberry liqueur
½ oz. lemon juice
Splash of lemon-lime soda

CLASSIC GIMLET

2½ oz. Skyy vodka
Juice of one fresh lime

Shake with ice. Serve in a chilled martini glass. Garnish with a lime wheel.

CLASSIC LEMON DROP

1½ parts Stolichnaya vodka
3 lemon squeezes, then discard
¾ part simple syrup

Shake vigorously with ice and strain into a chilled rocks glass rimmed with sugar. Garnish with a lemon wedge and serve.

CLASSIC MARTINI

3 oz. Teton Glacier potato vodka
Think of vermouth

CLIMAX

½ oz. vodka
½ oz. triple sec
½ oz. amaretto
½ oz. white crème de cacao
½ oz. banana liqueur
Milk or cream

Pour first five ingredients into a glass with ice and fill with milk or cream. Shake.

CLOUDY NIGHT

1 part vodka
1 part Tia Maria

Stir on the rocks.

COCA

¾ oz. vodka
¾ oz. Southern Comfort
¾ oz. black raspberry liqueur
1 oz. orange juice
1 oz. cranberry juice

Shake with ice and strain into a chilled glass.

COCO MARTINI

1½ oz. Three Olives vodka
2½ oz. Chocolate Martini Mixer
1 oz. crème de cacao

Shake over ice and strain into a chilled martini glass.

COCO POM

1½ oz. Smirnoff Red Label vodka
¼ oz. Captain Morgan Parrot Bay Coconut Rum
½ oz. pomegranate juice
1 tsp. coconut flakes

Shake first three ingredients with ice and strain into a chilled martini glass. Garnish with coconut flakes.

COCOA PEACH MARTINI

1½ oz. vodka
½ oz. Malibu
½ oz. peach schnapps
1½ oz. cranberry juice

Shake all ingredients with ice and strain into a chilled martini glass. Garnish with a slice of peach.

COCONUT APPLE CHOCOLATE DREAM CREAM MARTINI

1 oz. half-and-half
1 oz. Van Gogh chocolate liqueur
1 oz. Van Gogh coconut vodka
1 oz. Van Gogh Wild Appel vodka

Pour ingredients into a cocktail shaker. Add crushed ice and let stand for five seconds. Shake vigorously for five seconds and strain into a double martini glass.

COFFEE MARTINI

2½ oz. vanilla vodka
1½ oz. coffee liqueur
½ oz. chilled espresso coffee

Shake all ingredients with ice and strain into a chilled martini glass. Garnish with a chocolate-coated coffee bean.

COLLINS CLASSIC

2 oz. Three Olives vodka
1 tsp. powdered sugar
Splash of lemon juice
club soda

Shake first three ingredients with ice and strain into a glass with ice. Fill with club soda and stir. Garnish with a lemon wedge, an orange wedge, and a cherry.

COLORADO MOTHER

¾ oz. vodka
¾ oz. coffee liqueur
¾ oz. tequila
Milk or cream
Galliano

Pour first three ingredients into a glass over ice and fill with milk or cream. Shake. Top with Galliano.

COMFORTABLE SCREW

1 oz. vodka
1 oz. Southern Comfort
Orange juice

Pour first two ingredients into a glass with ice and fill with orange juice.

COOKIE DOUGH

2 oz. Stolichnaya Vanil vodka
3 oz. tonic

Mix ingredients with ice in a mixing glass. Pour into a tall glass.

COOL AID

¾ oz. vodka
¾ oz. melon liqueur
¾ oz. amaretto
Cranberry juice

Pour first four ingredients into a glass over ice. Fill with cranberry juice and shake.

COOL CITRON

1 oz. Absolut Citron vodka
½ oz. Hiram Walker white crème de menthe

Stir on the rocks.

COOLER

2 oz. Skyy vodka
1 tsp. sugar
Club soda

Pour first two ingredients into a glass and fill with club soda. Garnish with the peel of one lemon cut in a continuous spiral.

COPPERHEAD

2 oz. Skyy vodka
Ginger ale

Pour vodka into a glass and fill with ginger ale.

COSMOPOLITAN

2 oz. Skyy citrus vodka
½ oz. triple sec
Splash of cranberry juice
Squeeze of fresh lime
Lemon twist

COSMO KAZI

4 parts vodka
1 part triple sec
Dash of lime juice
Splash of cranberry juice

Build over ice.

COSSACK CHARGE

1½ oz. Sobieski vodka
½ oz. cognac
½ oz. cherry brandy

Shake or blend with cracked ice and pour into a chilled cocktail glass.

CRANBERRY SCREWDRIVER

1½ oz. Smirnoff Cranberry vodka
3 oz. orange juice

Stir well in a glass with ice.

CRANBERRY SEA BREEZE

2 oz. Smirnoff Cranberry vodka
2 oz. grapefruit juice
2 oz. cranberry juice

Stir well in a glass with ice. Garnish with a lemon twist.

CRAN-COSMO

2 parts UV Citruv vodka
1 part lime juice
1 part triple sec
1 part cranberry juice

Shake with ice and strain into a martini glass.

CRANPEPPAR

1¼ oz. Peppar vodka
Cranberry juice

Pour vodka over ice into a tall glass and fill with cranberry juice.

CRANTINI

2 oz. Skyy vodka
½ oz. triple sec
4 oz. cranberry juice

CRAZY BROAD

1 oz. vodka
1 oz. amaretto
1 oz. Southern Comfort
Cranberry juice
Ginger ale

Pour first three ingredients into a glass with ice. Fill with equal parts cranberry juice and ginger ale.

CREAMSICLE

1 part UV orange vodka
1 part cream
1 part triple sec
1 part orange juice

Serve over ice in a lowball glass.

CREAMSICLE FROZEN

1 oz. Three Olives cherry vodka
1 oz. Three Olives orange vodka
2 oz. orange juice
1 oz. milk or cream

Blend with a cup of ice until smooth. Garnish with a cherry.

Ⅎ CREAMSICLE

1½ oz. Ohranj vodka
½ oz. Irish cream

Serve on the rocks.

CRUSH

2 oz. Skyy citrus vodka
Orange juice
Splash of lemon-lime soda

Pour vodka into a glass and fill with orange juice. Top with a splash of lemon-lime soda.

CRUSHED ORANGE

1½ oz. Smirnoff orange vodka
2 oz. pineapple juice
2 oz. cranberry juice

Stir well with ice. Garnish with an orange slice.

CUPID'S PASSION

1 oz. Ciroc vodka
½ oz. Chambord
3 oz. cranberry juice

Shake with ice and strain into a martini glass. Garnish with a twist of lime.

CUPPA JOE MARTINI

¾ oz. Smirnoff Red Label vodka
¾ oz. hazelnut liqueur
1 oz. espresso (cold)

Shake well and serve in a chilled martini glass. Garnish with a lemon zest twist.

CUTTHROAT

1¼ oz. cranberry vodka, chilled
Orange juice

Pour cranberry vodka into a tall glass with ice. Fill with orange juice.

DAISY

2 oz. Skyy vodka
Juice of ½ lemon
½ tsp. powdered sugar
1 tsp. grenadine

DAISY CUTTER

1 oz. vodka (top)
½ oz. blue curacao (bottom)
½ oz. grenadine (bottom)
Lemon-lime soda

Pour first three ingredients into a shot glass and gently fill pint glass ¾ full with lemon-lime soda. Drop shot into pint glass.

DAMSEL IN DISTRESS

2 oz. Skyy citrus vodka
1 oz. coconut rum
Splash of orange juice
Splash of sour mix

DARK EYES

2 oz. vodka
¼ oz. Hiram Walker blackberry brandy
½ tsp. lime juice

Shake with ice and strain into a brandy snifter. Garnish with a lime slice or mint sprig.

DARK SIDE

1½ oz. vodka
1½ oz. brandy
1 oz. coffee liqueur
½ oz. White crème de menthe

Stir with ice.

DARK VANILLA

2 oz. Skyy Vanilla vodka
Drop of coffee liqueur

DAY SHIFT

7 parts Absolut Mandrin vodka
2 parts cranberry juice
2 parts soda water

Build in a chilled highball glass and garnish with an orange slice.

DEATH ROW

½ oz. vodka
½ oz. citrus vodka
½ oz. orange vodka
½ oz. orange liqueur
½ oz. amaretto
½ oz. sloe gin
Lemon-lime soda

Pour first four ingredients into a glass and shake with ice. Fill with lemon-lime soda.

DESERT SUNRISE

2 oz. Skyy vodka
1½ oz. orange juice
1½ oz. pineapple juice
Dash of grenadine

DEVIL'S TAIL

2 oz. Skyy vodka
2 oz. light rum
2 tsp. apricot brandy
½ tsp. fresh lime juice
2 tsp. grenadine
Lime twist

DIRTY ASHTRAY

½ oz. vodka
½ oz. gin
½ oz. rum
½ oz. tequila
½ oz. blue curacao
Dash grenadine
Pineapple juice
Sour mix

Pour first six ingredients into a glass with ice and fill with equal parts pineapple juice and sour mix. Shake. Garnish with a lemon.

DIRTY DOG

2 oz. Sobieski vodka
Grapefruit juice
Bitters

Pour vodka into a glass with ice and fill with grapefruit juice. Add 2 or 3 dashes of bitters.

DIRTY MARTINI

2 oz. Skyy vodka
¼ oz. olive juice

Stir. Serve in a chilled martini glass.

DIRTY MONKEY

¾ oz. vodka
¾ oz. coffee liqueur
¾ oz. banana liqueur
½ scoop vanilla ice cream

Blend until smooth.

DIVINE GODDESS

¾ oz. Chateau Pomari
1¼ oz. Three Olives vodka
2 oz. orange juice
3 oz. V8 Splash Tropical Blend

Blend with ice. Garnish with a chunk of mango.

DOUBLE O' SCREWDRIVER

2 oz. Skyy orange vodka
Orange juice

Pour vodka into a glass and fill with orange juice.

DOUBLE VANILLA

2 oz. Skyy vanilla vodka
Vanilla cola

Pour vodka into a glass and fill with vanilla cola. Garnish with a lemon twist.

DREAMSICLE

1½ oz. Skyy vanilla vodka
½ oz. Frangelico
½ oz. triple sec
Splash of cream

DRINK OF THE GODS

2 oz. Skyy vodka
1 oz. blueberry schnapps
1 oz. pineapple juice

DUBLIN DELIGHT

1½ oz. vodka
½ oz. Midori

Shake with ice and strain into an old-fashioned glass half filled with crushed ice. Garnish with a green maraschino cherry.

EARTHQUAKE

2 oz. Stoli
Dash blue curacao
Splash of lemon-lime soda

Pour into a rocks glass over ice.

ECSTASY

2 oz. Three Olives Grape vodka
¼ oz. grenadine
¼ oz. blue curacao
Splash of tonic

Shake with ice and strain into a chilled martini glass. Garnish with an orange slice.

ELECTRIC LEMONADE

1¼ oz. vodka
½ oz. blue curacao
2 oz. sweet & sour mix
Splash 7 Up

Flash blend, except 7Up, and pour over ice into a tall glass. Top with 7Up. Garnish with a lemon slice.

ELECTRIC PEACH

2 oz. vodka, chilled
¼ oz. peach schnapps
½ oz. cranberry juice cocktail
¼ oz. orange juice

ELIT CLASSIC MARTINI

1 part Stolichnaya Elit vodka
Splash of dry vermouth

Shake with ice and strain into a martini glass. Garnish with green olives.

ESPRESSO MARTINI

2 oz. Skyy vodka
1 oz. Tia Maria
2 oz. espresso coffee

ESSENTIALLY VOX

1 part Vox vodka
Dash of dry vermouth

Garnish with slices of lemon, lime, and orange.

FIRE

2 oz. Ohranj vodka
¼ oz. cinnamon schnapps

Serve on the rocks.

FIREFLY

2 oz. vodka
Grapefruit juice
Grenadine

Pour first two ingredients into a tall glass over ice. Add grenadine.

FIZZ

2 oz. Skyy vodka
Juice of lemon
Juice of lime
2 tsp. sugar
Club soda

Pour first four ingredients into a glass and fill with club soda.

FLORIDA JOY

1¼ oz. Absolut Citron vodka
½ oz. Hiram Walker triple sec

Mix with cracked ice in a shaker or blender and pour into a chilled highball glass. Garnish with a lemon slice.

FLUFFY CLOUD

1 oz. Three Olives vodka
1 oz. white crème de cacao
1 oz. cream

Shake with ice until foamy and strain into a martini glass.

FLYING GRASSHOPPER

1 oz. vodka
¾ oz. green crème de menthe
¾ oz. white crème de cacao
¼ oz. cream

Shake. Serve or strain into a chilled glass.

FORBIDDEN COFFEE

1 oz. Kahlua
1 oz. Yazi
4 oz. milk

FORBIDDEN CITY

1 oz. Calpico
1½ oz. Yazi
8 oz. seltzer water

FORBIDDEN FRUIT

1 part Vox green apple vodka
1 part Dekuyper Pucker sour apple schnapps
1 part pomegranate juice

Shake and strain into a martini glass.

FOUNTAIN OF FRUIT COCKTAIL

1½ oz. Three Olives vodka
½ oz. Cointreau
1 oz. sour mix
2 oz. pomegranate juice
Splash of lemon-lime soda

Shake first four ingredients and pour over ice into a cocktail glass. Top with lemon-lime soda and garnish with a lemon twist.

FRANKLY, MARY, I DON'T GIVE A CLAM

2 oz. Skyy vodka
6 oz. Clamato
2 tsp. Frank's Redhot Original Cayenne Pepper Sauce
1 tsp. fresh lemon juice
½ tsp. Worcestershire sauce

FROOTY BIZNESS MARTINI

1 oz. Three Olives vodka
1 oz. peach schnapps
3 oz. pineapple juice
3 oz. cranberry juice

Shake over ice and strain into a chilled martini glass. Garnish with a pineapple wedge and a cherry.

FROZEN CHERRY MARGARITA

1½ oz. Three Olives Cherry vodka
½ oz. triple sec
1 oz. lime juice
Splash grenadine

Blend with 2 cups crushed ice. Garnish with a lime wedge.

FROZEN RUSSIAN

1 oz. Baileys Irish cream
¼ oz. Smirnoff Red Label vodka
¼ oz. Godiva chocolate liqueur
2 scoops vanilla ice cream

Blend and serve in a hurricane glass.

FRUIT COCKTAIL

1 oz. Skyy melon vodka
1 oz. Skyy berry vodka
2 oz. cranberry juice
Splash of Cointreau

FRUIT FOUNTAIN

1 part Vox vodka
½ part DeKuyper Pucker sour apple schnapps
½ part DeKuyper Razzmatazz liqueur
½ part orange juice
Splash of 7 Up

FRUITS OF THE FOREST

1 part Vox vodka
Dash of simple syrup or lime juice
Fresh strawberries, raspberries, and blackberries
1 bunch of edible flowers (i.e., pansies, roses)

Muddle the berries in a mixing glass with a muddler. Add a dash of simple syrup and vodka and shake sharply. Pour into a tall glass with ice.

FUDGSICLE

2 oz. vodka, chilled
½ oz. crème de cacao
¼ oz. chocolate syrup

Shake with ice and serve on the rocks.

FUNNYBONE

1 oz. Three Olives Cherry vodka
1 oz. melon liqueur
2 oz. pineapple juice

Shake with ice and strain into a chilled martini glass. Garnish with a cherry.

FUZZY MARTINI

2 oz. Skyy vodka
1 oz. peach schnapps
Splash of orange juice

FUZZY NAVEL WITH VODKA

2 oz. Skyy vodka
1 oz. peach schnapps
Orange juice

Pour first two ingredients into a glass and fill with orange juice.

G'S MARTINI

2 oz. Three Olives Grape vodka
1 oz. Grand Marnier
Splash of grape juice

Shake with ice and strain into a chilled martini glass. Garnish with an orange slice.

GHOST

1¼ oz. Smirnoff Vanilla vodka
¼ oz. Godiva chocolate liqueur
¼ oz. half-and-half
¼ oz. simple syrup
¼ oz. shavings of white chocolate

Shake first four ingredients with ice and strain into a chilled martini glass rimmed with white chocolate. Garnish with white chocolate shavings.

GINGER SNAP LEMONADE

1½ oz. Smirnoff vodka
1 oz. Arrow ginger brandy
2 oz. pineapple juice
4 oz. lemonade

Stir. Garnish with a lemon twist.

GINGERLY VOX

1½ parts Vox vodka
1 part ginger liquor
1 thin banana leaf
Sliced fresh ginger

Mix in a shaker half-filled with ice.

GLAMOROUS MARTINI

2 oz. Skyy vodka
¼ oz. orange juice
¼ oz. grapefruit juice
Splash of Cointreau

GLASS SLIPPER

1 part Smirnoff vodka
¾ part coffee liqueur
¼ part Cointreau

Stir over ice.

GLASS TOWER

1 oz. vodka
1 oz. light rum
½ oz. Cointreau
½ oz. peach schnapps
½ oz. Sambuca
Lemon-lime soda

Pour first five ingredients into a glass with ice. Fill with lemon-lime soda.
Garnish with a lime.

GODCHILD

2 oz. Sobieski vodka
1 oz. amaretto
1 oz. heavy cream

GODMOTHER

2 oz. Sobieski vodka
¾ oz. amaretto

GOLFER

1 oz. Absolut Citron vodka
½ oz. Bombay gin
¼ oz. Martini & Rossi extra-dry vermouth

Serve on the rocks with a twist of lemon peel.

GOOD N' GLACIER

2 oz. Teton Glacier potato vodka
1 tbsp. Pernod

Shake with ice and serve up in a chilled martini glass.

GORKY PARK

2 oz. vodka
1 tsp. grenadine
Dash orange bitters

Combine in a shaker with crushed ice, or blend. Strain into a chilled cocktail glass. Garnish with half a strawberry.

GRAND FINALE

2 oz. Skyy vodka
1 oz. cognac

Stir on the rocks.

GRAND ROYAL

2 oz. Absolut vodka
4 dashes of Goldschlager liqueur
2 oz. champagne

Build in a champagne glass—make sure to include gold flakes from the Goldschlager!

GRAPE APE

1 part UV Grape vodka
1 part lemon-lime soda
Splash of sweet & sour mix

Serve over ice in a highball glass.

GRAPE CRUSH

2 oz. Three Olives grape vodka
1 oz. Cointreau
Splash of orange juice

Shake with ice and strain into a chilled martini glass. Garnish with an orange slice.

GRAPE CRUSH II

1 oz. vodka
1 oz. black raspberry liqueur
2 oz. sour mix
1 oz. 7 Up

Serve over ice in Collins glass. Garnish with an orange or a cherry.

GRAPE GROOVE

1 part UV Grape vodka
1 part Chambord
1 part pineapple juice
1 part lemon-lime soda

Serve over ice in a highball glass.

GRAPE NUT MARTINI

2 oz. Three Olives grape vodka
1 oz. amaretto

Shake with ice and strain into a chilled martini glass.

GRAPETINI

1 part UV Grape vodka
1 part lemonade
Splash of triple sec

Shake with ice and strain into a martini glass.

GRASSHOPPER COCKTAIL

1 oz. Skyy vodka
½ oz. green crème de menthe
½ oz. white crème de cacao
Splash of half-and-half

Garnish with a candy cane.

GREEN APPLE VODKA & SODA

2 oz. Smirnoff green apple vodka
3 oz. soda

Build over ice and garnish with a slice of lime.

GREEN EYES

1⅓ oz. Sobieski vodka
⅔ oz. blue curacao
1 oz. fresh orange juice

Pour all ingredients into a shaker with ice. Shake. Strain into a cocktail glass.

GREEN GRAPE

2 oz. Three Olives Grape vodka
1 oz. melon liqueur
Splash of pineapple juice

Shake with ice and strain into a chilled martini glass. Garnish with an orange slice.

GREEN HORNET

2 oz. vodka, chilled
¼ oz. Midori
½ oz. sweet & sour mix

GREEN SNEAKER

1 oz. vodka
½ oz. Midori
½ oz. triple sec
2 oz. orange juice

Stir with ice, strain, and serve straight up.

GREMLIN

1½ oz. vodka
¾ oz. blue curacao
¾ oz. rum
½ oz. orange juice

Shake with ice, strain, and serve straight up.

GREYHOUND

2 oz. Sobieski vodka
Grapefruit juice

Pour vodka into a tall glass over crushed ice and fill with grapefruit juice.

GUAVA

2 oz. Smirnoff vodka
6 oz. Hawaiian guava fruit juice
1 tsp. fresh lime juice
¼ lime wedge

Pour first three ingredients into a glass over ice. Squeeze lime juice and rub on the rim of the glass. Drop in for garnish.

HANDBALL COOLER

2 oz. Skyy vodka
Club soda
Splash of orange juice

HARRY ORANGE

2 oz. Skyy orange vodka
Orange juice
Splash of grenadine

Pour vodka into a glass and fill with orange juice. Top with a splash of grenadine.

HARVEY WALLBANGER CLASSIC

2 oz. Three Olives vodka
4 oz. orange juice
¾ oz. Galliano

Mix first two ingredients in a glass with ice. Sprinkle Galliano on top and garnish with an orange wedge.

HAWAIIAN PIPELINE

1½ oz. pineapple vodka, chilled
2 oz. orange juice
1 oz. cranberry juice

Shake and serve over ice.

HAWAII FIVE-O

1½ oz. pineapple vodka, chilled
¼ oz. blue curacao

Shake and pour into a hurricane glass with ice. Garnish with pineapple spear, cherry, and umbrella.

HEARTTHROB

1¼ oz. cranberry vodka, chilled
¼ oz. peach schnapps
¼ oz. grapefruit juice

Shake and pour into a tall glass with ice.

HOLIDAY LIGHTS SHOOTER

½ oz. Skyy vanilla vodka
½ oz. Goldschlager

HOLLYWOOD

2 oz. Sobieski vodka
1 oz. black raspberry liqueur
Cranberry juice

Pour first two ingredients into a tall glass with ice and fill with cranberry juice.

HOLLYWOOD BABYLON

2 oz. Skyy vodka
Splash of fresh raspberry puree

HONEYDEW

2 oz. Skyy Vanilla vodka
1 oz. Midori melon liqueur
Splash of lemon-lime soda

HOP-SKIP-AND-GO-NAKED

1 oz. Grey Goose vodka
1 oz. Bombay gin
Juice of ½ lime
Budweiser

Pour first three ingredients into a mug over ice. Fill with Budweiser.

HORSESHOT

1¼ oz. Sobieski vodka
4 oz. tomato juice
1¼ oz. horseradish

Serve over ice in a cocktail glass. Garnish with a celery stalk.

HOT APPLETINI

2 oz. Skyy vodka
1 oz. sour apple liqueur
Splash of cinnamon liqueur

HOT LIPS

2 oz. cranberry vodka, chilled
¼ oz. Goldschlager

HOT MARTINI

2 oz. Three Olives vodka
Splash dry vermouth

Stir gently for 15 seconds then shake with ice and strain into a martini glass. Garnish with 3 drops Tabasco sauce, olives, or jalapenos.

HULA-HOOP

2 oz. Absolut vodka, chilled
1 oz. pineapple juice
½ oz. orange juice

I AM COOKIE!

3 parts Absolut vodka
4 parts blood orange juice
1 part chocolate cookie
3 parts red food coloring
Cinnamon stick
Dash cinnamon

Shake with ice and strain into a chilled highball glass.

ICE PICK

1¼ oz. Sobieski vodka
Lemon iced tea

Pour over ice in a tall glass. Garnish with a slice of lemon.

IMPERIAL CZAR

¼ oz. Smirnoff vodka
¼ oz. triple sec
¾ oz. dry sparkling wine
Dash lime juice
Dash orange bitters

Combine in a shaker, except wine. Strain into a chilled wine glass. Add wine, stir.

IRISH MARTINI

2 oz. Teton Glacier potato vodka
1 oz. Baileys Irish cream

IRISH QUAALUDE #1

½ oz. vodka
½ oz. Irish cream
½ oz. coffee liqueur
½ oz. hazelnut liqueur

Shake with ice, strain, and serve straight up.

IRON BUTTERFLY

¾ oz. Grey Goose vodka
¾ oz. coffee liqueur
¾ oz. Irish cream

Shake with ice, strain, and serve straight up.

ISLAND TEA

1½ oz. vodka
1 oz. grenadine
1 tsp. lemon juice

Shake with ice and strain over ice in an old-fashioned glass. Garnish with a mint sprig.

ITALIAN SCREWDRIVER

2 oz. Skyy vodka
Splash of lemon juice
3 oz. orange juice
2 oz. grapefruit juice
Splash ginger ale

JACKIE-O MARTINI

2 oz. Skyy vodka
Splash of apricot brandy
Dash of grenadine
⅓ oz. pineapple juice

JERICHO'S BREEZE

2 oz. Skyy vodka
¾ oz. blue curacao
2 oz. sour mix
Splash lemon-lime soda
Splash orange juice

JULIUS

2 oz. Skyy Vanilla vodka
4 oz. orange juice
½ oz. white crème de cacao
Splash of cream

JUNGLE GARDENIA

1 part Smirnoff vodka
1 part crème de banana
1 part milk

Serve over ice.

JUPITER JUICE

1½ Stoli
Splash triple sec
Splash lime juice
Splash grenadine

Serve straight up on the rocks.

KAMIKAZE

1 oz. Skyy vodka
¼ oz. Cointreau
¼ oz. lime juice

Shake with ice. Serve in a shot glass.

KAMIKAZE SHOT

1 oz. Three Olives vodka
¼ oz. Triple Sec
1 oz. sour mix
Splash of lime juice

Shake with ice and strain into a shot glass.

KATT'S MEOW CLASSIC

1½ oz. Three Olives vodka
½ oz. triple sec
2 oz. sour mix
2 oz. lemon-lime soda

Mix in a glass with ice.

KAYTUSHA ROCKET

1 oz. vodka
½ oz. coffee liqueur
Dash of cream
1 oz. pineapple juice

Shake with ice, strain into a glass, and serve straight up.

KBG

½ oz. Kremlyovskaya chocolate vodka
½ oz. Grand Marnier
½ oz. Bailey's Irish cream

Serve on the rocks, with coffee, or as a shooter.

KISS (KREMLYOVSKAYA IS SO SWEET)

1 oz. Kremlyovskaya
½ oz. half-and-half
1½ oz. Baileys Irish cream

Shake with ice. Float Baileys. Garnish with a maraschino cherry.

KNOCKOUT PUNCH

2 oz. Kremlyovskaya chocolate vodka
2 oz. cream

Shake. Serve over ice or straight up.

KISSABLE

¾ oz. Smirnoff orange vodka
¾ oz. white crème de cacao
1½ oz. milk

Shake and strain into a martini glass.

KOOL-AID

1 oz. Sobieski vodka
1 oz. honeydew melon liqueur
2 oz. cranberry juice

Build over ice in a rocks glass.

KREM DE LA KREM

1 oz. Kremlyovskaya chocolate vodka
½ oz. green crème de menthe
½ oz. white crème de cacao
Vanilla ice cream

Blend with ice. Top with a mint leaf and a chocolate stick for garnish.

KREMIN GLACIER MARTINI

1 oz. Kremlyovkska vodka
1 oz. Bombay Sapphire gin
Splash of blue curacao

Serve in a well-chilled martini glass. Garnish with an orange slice.

KREMLIN COLONEL

2 oz. vodka
2 tbsp. sugar syrup

Combine in a shaker with ice. Strain into a cocktail glass. Garnish with 3 to 4 mint leaves torn in half.

KREMLYOVSKAYA RASPBERRY RUMBLE

1½ oz. Kremlyovskaya chocolate vodka
½ oz. Kahlua
¾ oz. Chambord
½ oz. Tuaca
Cream or half-and-half

Build the first four ingredients in a Collins glass with crushed ice. Fill with cream or half-and-half and stir gently. Garnish with milk chocolate shavings.

KRETCHMA

1 oz. Smirnoff vodka
1 oz. crème de cacao
½ oz. lemon juice
½ tsp. grenadine

Shake or blend with cracked ice and strain into a chilled cocktail glass.

KURANT AFFAIR

1¼ oz. Absolut Kurant vodka
Cranberry juice
Club soda

Pour vodka over ice in a tall glass. Fill most of the way with cranberry juice. Top off with a splash of soda. Garnish with a wedge of lime.

KURANT AND 7 UP

1¼ oz. Absolut Kurant vodka
7-Up

Pour vodka in a tall glass over ice and fill with 7 Up. Garnish with a slice of lemon and a slice of lime.

KURANT JUICE BREAK

1½ oz. Absolut Kurant vodka
2 oz. orange juice
2 oz. pineapple juice
½ oz. Grand Marnier

Mix with cracked ice in a shaker or blender. Pour into chilled cooler glass. Garnish with orange slice and a cherry.

KURANT ORCHARD

1½ oz. Absolut Kurant vodka
4 oz. grapefruit juice
½ oz. apple brandy
1 tsp. Grand Marnier

Mix all ingredients, except Grand Marnier, with cracked ice in a blender or shaker. Pour into chilled Collins glass. Float Grand Marnier on top.

KURITA

1 oz. Absolut Kurant vodka
½ oz. Cointreau
Juice of a small lime

Mix with ice and strain into a cocktail glass. Garnish with a slice of lime.

LAID-BACK LEMONADE CLASSIC

1½ oz. Three Olives vodka
½ oz. orange juice
¼ oz. fresh lemon juice
¼ oz. grapefruit juice (optional)
½ tsp. sugar

Mix ingredients in a tall Collins glass filled with ice. Top with club soda and garnish with an orange slice.

LAST ROUND

2 oz. Kremlyovskaya chocolate vodka
¼ oz. Frangelico

Serve straight up, as a shot, or as a martini.

LA LYCHEE MARTINI

1½ oz. Three Olives vodka
1½ oz. Hakusan raspberry saki
1 oz. lychee juice

Shake with ice and strain into a chilled martini glass. Garnish with fresh raspberries and lychees.

L.A. SUNRISE

2 oz. Skyy vodka
½ oz. crème de banana
1 oz. orange juice
1 oz. pineapple juice
¼ oz. rum

LEMON CHI CHI

1½ oz. vodka
1½ oz. sweet & sour mix
2–3 oz. pina colada mix
1½ oz. pineapple juice

Blend with crushed ice and serve in a 15 oz. glass.

LEMON CHIFFON

2 oz. vodka, chilled
¼ oz. triple sec
1 oz. sweet & sour mix

Squeeze and drop in a fresh lemon wedge.

LEMON DROP

2 oz. Skyy citrus vodka
1 oz. fresh lemon juice
Splash of Cointreau

LEMON DROP II

2 oz. vodka
2 oz. sweet & sour mix
Splash of 7 Up
Splash of club soda

Serve in a tall glass with ice.

LEMON ICE

1¼ oz. Sobieski vodka
½ oz. Cointreau
1½ oz. sweet & sour mix
½ oz. lemon juice
7 Up

Build over iced and fill with 7 Up in a 15 oz. glass. Garnish with lemon slice.

LEMON MERINGUE PIE

2 oz. Skyy vodka
1 oz. fresh lemon juice
Splash of Cointreau
Splash of cream

Shake with ice. Serve in a chilled martini glass.

LEMON MERINGUE PIE II

2 parts Vox vodka
1 part Licor 43
Splash of sweetened lemonade concentrate
Whipped cream
Powdered graham crackers

Shake first three ingredients with ice and strain into a glass. Garnish with whipped cream and graham crackers.

LIMONGRAD

1½ oz. Stolichnaya Limonnaya vodka
3–4 oz. cranberry juice

Serve in 5 oz. rocks glass over ice.

LIQUID CITRUS

1½ oz. Skyy citrus vodka
1 oz. cranberry juice
½ oz. sour apple liqueur
Splash of sweet & sour

LONDON BREEZE

2 oz. Vodka 02, chilled
Muscadet wine
Frozen white seedless grapes

Pour first two ingredients into a glass filled with frozen grapes.

LO'S VALIUM

2 oz. vodka
½ oz. Godiva chocolate liqueur
½ oz. DeKuyper Peachtree schnapps

Serve in a chilled sugar-rimmed martini glass.

LOVE GODDESS

2 oz. Three Olives vodka
1 oz. pomegranate juice
2 oz. ginger ale

Pour ingredients over ice into a highball glass. Garnish with a slice of orange.

LUNAR BREEZE

Equal parts:
Stoli
Cranberry juice
Grapefruit juice

Mix in a tall glass over ice.

LYCHEE DAIQUIRI

2 oz. lychee fruit (canned)
1 oz. lychee juice
2 oz. Yazi

Blend or serve over ice.

MACHETE

1½ oz. Smirnoff vodka
⅔ glass pineapple juice
Tonic

Pour first two ingredients into a glass and fill with tonic. Stir.

MADAME ROXANE

2 oz. Three Olives vodka
1½ oz. cranberry juice
1½ oz. pineapple juice
Sparkling wine

Shake first three ingredients with ice and strain into a chilled martini glass. Top with sparkling wine.

MADRAS

1¼ oz. vodka
Cranberry juice
Orange juice

Pour vodka into a tall glass over ice and fill with equal parts orange juice and cranberry juice.

MAGNIFICENT MELON

1½ part Vox vodka
1 part DeKuyper melon liqueur
Splash of pineapple juice

Mix in a shaker half-filled with ice. Garnish with pineapple leaves, watermelon, honeydew, and cantaloupe.

MALIOOO MARTINI

3 oz. Teton Glacier potato vodka
1 tbsp. rum
1 tbsp. orange juice
1 tbsp. pineapple juice

MALIBU RAIN

2 oz. vodka, chilled
1½ oz. pineapple juice
½ oz. Malibu
Splash of orange juice

MAMA'S MARTINI

3 oz. vanilla vodka
½ oz. apricot brandy
5 dashes of Angostura bitters
5 dashes of freshly squeezed lemon juice

Shake all ingredients with ice and strain into a chilled martini glass. Garnish with a lemon twist.

MANGO COCONUT BLUEBERRY CLEAR COSMO

½ oz. blueberry liqueur
¼ oz. Van Gogh Citroen vodka
1 oz. Van Gogh Coconut vodka
1 oz. Van Gogh Mango vodka
½ oz. Van Gogh Triple Sec 30 liqueur
1 oz. white cranberry juice

Pour ingredients into a cocktail shaker. Add crushed ice and let stand for five seconds. Shake vigorously for five seconds and strain into a double martini glass. Garnish with a mango slice or a coconut chunk and a red maraschino cherry.

MANGO COCONUT HAZELNUT CLEAR COSMO

½ oz. hazelnut liqueur
¼ oz. Van Gogh Citroen vodka
1 oz. Van Gogh coconut vodka
1 oz. Van Gogh mango vodka
½ oz. Van Gogh Triple Sec 30 liqueur
1 oz. white cranberry juice

Pour ingredients into a cocktail shaker. Add crushed ice and let stand for five seconds. Shake vigorously for five seconds and strain into a double martini glass. Garnish with a mango slice or a coconut chunk and a red maraschino cherry.

MARGARITA

2 oz. Absolut Kurant vodka
½ oz. orange liqueur
Juice of small lime

Shake with ice and strain into a cocktail glass. Garnish with a slice of lime.

MARION BOBCAT

2 oz. Smirnoff vodka
3 oz. orange juice
3 oz. lemon lime seltzer
1 dash bitters
¼ lime wedge

Pour first four ingredients into a tall glass over ice. Squeeze lime into glass and drop in for garnish.

MARS MARY

2 oz. Stoli
6 oz. tomato juice
½ oz. horseradish
Lemon, salt, and pepper to taste

Pour first three ingredients over ice, add squeeze of lemon, salt, and pepper to taste. Shake and garnish with a celery stick.

MARTINI (VODKA)

2¼ oz. vodka
Dash of extra-dry vermouth

Shake or stir well over ice and strain into a cocktail glass straight up or over ice. Garnish with a twist or an olive.

MARTINI BOPPER

3 oz. Three Olives Cherry vodka
Splash of grenadine

Shake with ice and strain into a chilled martini glass. Garnish with a lime wedge.

MEAT AND POTATO MARTINI

2½ oz. Teton Glacier potato vodka
Splash dry vermouth

Shake with ice and strain into a martini glass. Garnish with a slice of sausage or pepperoni.

MEDITERRANEAN MARTINI

2 oz. Three Olives Pomegranate vodka
1 oz. Chateau Pomari pomegranate liqueur

Shake with ice and strain into a chilled martini glass. Garnish with a wedge of lime.

MELLOW ORANGE

2 oz. Grand Marnier
1 oz. Stoli vanilla vodka
1 oz. orange juice

Combine in a glass filled with ice.

MELONADE

2 oz. Skyy melon vodka
2 oz. pineapple juice
½ oz. grenadine

Serve in a tall glass with ice.

MELON-GIZER

2 oz. Skyy melon vodka
3 oz. energy drink

Serve in a tall glass with ice.

MELONTINI

2 oz. Skyy vodka
1 oz. Midori
Splash of lemon-lime soda

MELON BALL

½ oz. vodka
1 oz. honeydew melon liqueur
Orange juice
Pineapple juice

Pour first two ingredients into a glass over ice and fill with equal parts orange juice and pineapple juice.

MELROSE MARTINI

2 oz. Skyy citrus vodka
1 oz. orange juice
1 oz. orange brandy

MELON BALL POPPER

2 oz. Skyy melon vodka, chilled
Splash of lemon-lime soda

MELON BERRY

2 oz. Skyy berry vodka
1 oz. Midori melon liqueur
Splash of lemon-lime soda

MELON COSMO

2 oz. Skyy melon vodka
½ oz. Cointreau
Splash of cranberry juice

MELON CUCUMBER-TINI

2 oz. Skyy melon vodka
Fresh cucumber muddled over ice
½ oz. simple syrup

Serve in a chilled martini glass.

MELON DROP MARTINI

2 oz. Skyy melon vodka
2 oz. fresh lemon juice
Splash of sweet & sour
Splash of triple sec

Shake with ice. Serve in a chilled martini glass.

MELON MARGARITA

2 oz. Skyy melon vodka
Juice from 2 limes
½ oz. Cointreau
Splash of orange curacao

Shake with ice. Serve in a tall martini glass.

MELON MARTINI

2 oz. Skyy melon vodka
3 fresh watermelon cubes
Splash of lemon-lime soda

Serve over ice.

MELON MOJITO

2 oz. Skyy melon vodka
Fresh mint leaves
Spoonful of sugar
4 oz. soda water
Lime juice

Serve in a tall glass with ice.

MELON MOJO

2 oz. Skyy melon vodka
4 oz. fresh orange juice

Serve in a tall glass with ice.

MELON PIT MARTINI

2 oz. Skyy melon vodka
½ oz. amaretto
Splash of orange juice
Splash of lemon-lime soda
Raspberry liqueur

Float raspberry liqueur on the bottom.

MELON PRESS

2 oz. Skyy melon vodka
Soda
Lemon-lime soda

Pour vodka into a glass and fill with equal parts soda and lemon-lime soda.

MELON RISING

2 oz. Skyy melon vodka
Orange juice
Pineapple juice
Dash of grenadine

Pour vodka into a glass and fill with equal parts orange juice, and pineapple juice. Top with a dash of grenadine.

MELON TART

2 oz. Skyy melon vodka
¼ oz. lime juice
Sour mix
Lemon-lime soda
Splash of sour mix and lemon-lime soda

MERRY MARTINI

2 oz. Skyy vodka
¼ oz. Grand Marnier
Cranberry juice

Pour first two ingredients into a glass. Add enough cranberry juice to give drink a pink color.

MET MOJITO COCKTAIL

1 ¾ oz. Three Olives vodka
½ oz. Midori
¾ oz. lime juice
1 oz. simple syrup
Club soda
8–10 mint leaves

Pour first two ingredients into a glass over ice. In a pilsner glass, muddle the mint leaves, lime juice, and simple syrup, then add to glass. Top with club soda and garnish with mint.

MIAMI SHADES

1 oz. Ohranj vodka
¼ oz. peach schnapps
2 oz. grapefruit juice

Serve over ice.

MIDNIGHT ORCHID

1½ oz. cranberry vodka, chilled
¼ oz. Chambord
2 oz. pineapple juice
½ oz. half-and-half

Shake and strain over crushed ice or blend with ice.

MIDORI MISTLETOE PUNCH

1 part Skyy vodka
1 part champagne
1 part Midori
2 parts pineapple juice
1 part soda water

Prepare in a punch bowl, pour over ice. Garnish with mistletoe or a candy cane.

MIKHAIL'S MARTINI

2 oz. Stolichnaya Kafya vodka
½ oz. Stolichnaya Vanil vodka
Three coffee beans

Pour first two ingredients over ice in a large mixing glass or cocktail shaker. Stir and strain into a chilled martini glass. Add coffee beans.

MIND ERASER

1 oz. vodka
1 oz. coffee liqueur
Soda water

Pour first two ingredients into a glass over ice. Fill with soda water and serve with a straw.

MINTY LEMONADE

2 oz. Smirnoff vodka
1 tsp. green crème de menthe
4 oz. lemonade

Stir and garnish with a sprig of mint.

MISTLETOE MOJITO

2 oz. Skyy melon vodka
Fresh mint leaves
Spoonful of sugar
4 oz. soda water
Lime juice

MONKEY MARTINI

2 oz. Skyy vodka
Splash of banana liqueur
1½ oz. cranberry juice

MONSOON

¼ oz. vodka
¼ oz. coffee liqueur
¼ oz. amaretto
¼ oz. Irish cream
¼ oz. hazelnut liqueur

Serve in a shot glass.

MONSTER

2 oz. Skyy vodka
1 oz. Midori melon liqueur
Splash of pineapple juice

MOSCOW CHILL

2 oz. vodka
4 oz. Dr. Pepper

Pour vodka over shaved ice into a champagne glass and fill with Dr. Pepper. Garnish with a lime wedge.

MOUNT RUSHMORE SHOT

¾ oz. Three Olives vodka
1½ oz. Mountain Dew

Shake with ice and strain into a shot glass. Follow with a cherry.

MUDSLIDE

1 oz. Skyy vodka
1 oz. coffee liqueur
1 oz. Carolans Irish cream liqueur

Shake with ice. Serve over rocks.

NATURAL SELECTION

1 oz. Skyy berry vodka
¾ oz. apple pucker
¾ oz. Hypnotiq
Splash of pineapple juice

NAVALTINI

1 part UV Orange vodka
1 part champagne
1 part orange juice

Shake with ice and strain into a martini glass.

NEGRONI

2 oz. Skyy vodka
1 oz. Campari
Splash of Cinzano Red vermouth

Shake. Serve straight up in a martini glass or on the rocks.

NEVA

1½ oz. vodka
½ oz. tomato juice
½ oz. orange juice

Shake and strain into a stemmed glass over ice.

NEW YEAR CHEER

1 oz. Skyy Vanilla vodka
1 oz. amaretto
1 oz. fresh orange juice

Shake with ice. Serve on the rocks or straight up in a martini glass.

NEW YEAR'S EVE

2 oz. Skyy vodka
1 oz. hazelnut liqueur
1 oz. Carolans Irish cream

NUT HOUSE

2 oz. cranberry vodka, chilled
¼ oz. amaretto

Shake with ice. Serve straight up or on the rocks.

NUTS AND BERRIES

1 oz. Sobieski vodka
½ oz. hazelnut liqueur
½ oz. coffee liqueur
¼ oz. cream

Shake with ice and strain straight up into a 4 oz. rocks glass.

NUTCRACKER'S DREAM

1½ oz. Skyy berry vodka
1 tsp. maraschino cherry juice
6 oz. Brut champagne

OHRANJ BLOSSOM

1 oz. Stolichnaya Ohranj vodka
1 oz. Amaretto Disaronno
2 oz. orange juice
Dash lemon juice

Mix all ingredients with cracked ice in a blender or shaker and serve in a chilled old fashioned glass with several ice cubes.

OHRANJ JULIUS

¾ oz. Ohranj vodka
¾ oz. Cointreau
½ oz. orange juice
Mr. & Mrs. T's Sweet & Sour Mix

Mix first two ingredients in a glass with ½ oz. Mr. & Mrs. T's Sweet & Sour Mix and ½ oz. orange juice over crushed ice. Garnish with an orange slice.

OLD BLUE EYES

2 oz. Skyy vodka
1 oz. blue curacao
Splash of orange juice

Shake. Serve on the rocks.

OLIVER MARTINI

2½ oz. Three Olives vodka
Splash of olive juice

Stir gently over ice for 15 minutes. Strain into a chilled martini glass. Garnish with olives.

OP

2 oz. Skyy orange vodka
2 oz. pomegranate juice
Lemon-lime soda

Pour first two ingredients into a glass and fill with lemon-lime soda.

ORANGE BLISS

1½ oz. Skyy orange vodka
1 oz. Grand Marnier
3½ oz. orange juice

Serve in a tall glass with ice.

ORANGE BLOSSOM SPECIAL

2 oz. Three Olives Orange Vodka Shake
½ oz. triple sec
3 oz. sour mix

Shake with ice and strain into a sugar-rimmed martini glass. Garnish with an orange wedge and a cherry.

ORANGE & CAMPARI

2 oz. Skyy orange vodka
1 oz. Campari
Splash of simple syrup

ORANGE COCONUT AMSTERDAM SNOWTINI

½ oz. Van Gogh chocolate liqueur
1 oz. Van Gogh coconut vodka
1 oz. Van Gogh Oranje vodka

Prepare 1 cup of shaved ice. Combine vodka and syrup in small glass and stir. Pour mixture over shaved ice into a sherbet glass. Garnish with a red maraschino cherry and a cocktail umbrella. Have teaspoon available for use.

ORANGE COSMO

2 oz. Skyy orange vodka
1 oz. Cointreau
Splash of red cranberry juice
Squeeze of fresh lime

Shake with ice. Serve on the rocks or in a chilled martini glass.

ORANGE CRUSH

1¼ oz. Sobieski vodka
¾ oz. Cointreau
2 oz. orange juice

Shake with ice and strain into a glass.

ORANGE DROP

2 oz. Skyy orange vodka
½–1 oz. fresh lemon juice
Splash of simple syrup

Shake with ice. Serve on the rocks or in a chilled martini glass.

ORANGE ENERGIZER

2 oz. Skyy orange vodka
Energy drink

Pour vodka into a glass and fill with any energy drink.

ORANGE FUSION

¾ oz. Smirnoff orange vodka
¾ oz. peach schnapps

Shake with ice and strain into a shot glass.

ORANGE GINGER

2 oz. Skyy orange vodka
1 oz. lemon juice
Splash of triple sec
Ginger ale

Pour first two ingredients into a glass and fill with ginger ale. Top with a splash of triple sec.

ORANGE JAXX

2 oz. Skyy orange vodka
1 oz. DeKuyper Pucker sour apple
Slight splash of cinnamon liqueur

Shake with ice. Serve on the rocks or in a chilled martini glass.

ORANGE JULIUS

1½ oz. Skyy vanilla vodka
2 oz. fresh orange juice
Splash of cream

Shake with ice. Serve on the rocks or in a chilled martini glass.

ORANGE LUAU

2 oz. Skyy orange vodka
1 oz. apricot brandy
Orange juice
Pineapple juice

Pour first two ingredients into a glass and fill with equal parts orange juice and pineapple juice.

ORANGE MADRAS

2 oz. Skyy orange vodka
Cranberry juice
Orange juice
Pineapple juice

Pour vodka into a glass and fill with equal parts cranberry juice and orange juice.

ORANGE OC

2 oz. Skyy orange vodka
1 oz. mango juice
Splash of Cointreau
Splash of fresh lime juice
Dash of sugar

ORANGE PASSIONTINI

2 oz. Skyy orange vodka
½ oz. raspberry liqueur
1 oz. passion fruit juice

ORANGE QUENCH

2 oz. Skyy orange vodka
Fresh pomegranate juice
Splash of triple sec

ORANGE SEABREEZE

2 oz. Skyy orange vodka
Cranberry juice
Grapefruit juice

Pour vodka into a glass and fill with equal parts cranberry juice and grapefruit juice.

ORANGE SUNDOWNER

2 oz. Skyy orange vodka
1 oz. guava juice
½ oz. raspberry liqueur

ORANGE TRAFFIC LIGHT

1 oz. Skyy orange vodka
½ oz. sloe gin
¼ oz. grenadine
2 oz. orange juice
½ oz. Midori melon liqueur

ORANGE YEAH

2 oz. Skyy orange vodka
½ oz. apricot brandy
Cranberry juice

Pour first two ingredients into a glass and fill with cranberry juice.

ORANGUTAN

1 part UV Orange vodka
3 parts lemon-lime soda

Serve over ice in a highball glass.

ORCHID

2 oz. Skyy vodka
Dash of grenadine
1 oz. blue curacao
Splash of cranberry juice

OUTRIGGER

1 oz. Absolut Peppar vodka
½ oz. peach schnapps
Dash of lime juice
2 oz. pineapple juice

Shake with ice and strain into an old-fashioned glass over ice.

OYSTER SHOOTER

1 oz. Absolut Peppar vodka
1 raw oyster
Spoonful cocktail sauce
1 squeeze of lemon

Serve in a small rocks glass. It calls for a dash of horseradish, too, for those who dare.

PALM BEACH SUNSET

1½ oz. Skyy vodka
1 oz. amaretto
4 oz. orange juice
Splash of grenadine

PAMIR PEACH

1 oz. Stolichnaya Persik vodka
1 oz. Amaretto Disaronno
2 oz. orange juice
Dash lemon juice

Mix all ingredients with cracked ice in a blender or shaker and serve in a chilled old-fashioned glass with several ice cubes.

PAR 19

1½ oz. Absolut Citron vodka
Grape juice
Ginger ale

Pour vodka into a tall glass with ice and fill with half ginger ale and half grape juice.

PARTY FAVOR

2 oz. Skyy vodka
Splash of cranberry juice
⅓ oz. Midori melon liqueur
⅓ oz. amaretto
1 twist of lemon

PEACH AND CHONG

2 oz. Teton Glacier potato vodka
½ oz. peach schnapps
½ oz. Cointreau

Serve on the rocks with a fortune cookie.

PEACHES AND CREAM

½ part Vox vodka
1 part DeKuyper Peachtree schnapps
1 part cream

PEACH BLOSSOM

2 oz. Ciroc vodka
½ oz. peach puree

Shake with crushed ice and strain into a cocktail glass. Garnish with a peach slice.

PEACH BLOSSOM MARTINI

2½ oz. peach vodka
½ oz. red Dubonnet
½ oz. maraschino liqueur

Shake all ingredients with ice and strain into a chilled martini glass. Garnish with a thin slice of peach.

PEACH FUZZ

2 oz. Smirnoff vodka
½ oz. peach schnapps
3 oz. cranberry juice
3 oz. orange juice

Pour into a tall glass over ice. Garnish with an orange slice.

PEPPER MANHATTAN

2½ oz. Absolut Peppar vodka
½ oz. sweet vermouth

Shake with ice and strain into a stemmed glass. Garnish with a cherry.

PEPPAR SALTY DOG

1½ oz. Absolut Peppar vodka
Grapefruit juice

Salt the rim of a rocks glass. Pour in vodka over ice and fill with grape-fruit juice.

PEPPERMINT KISS

Cup of hot chocolate
½ part Vox vodka
1 part DeKuyper peppermint schnapps

Stir together in a pitcher.

PEPPERTINI

1½ oz. Absolut Peppar vodka
½ oz. vermouth

Shake over ice, stir, and pour into a rocks glass. Garnish with an olive.

PERFECT COSMO

1 part Stolichnaya vodka
½ part orange liqueur
1 part cranberry juice
1 lime squeeze, then discard
¼ part simple syrup

PERFECT MARTINI

2 oz. Skyy vodka
Dash of Cinzano Dry vermouth
Dash of Cinzano Sweet vermouth

PETRIFIER

2 oz. Sobieski vodka
2 oz. gin
2 oz. cognac
2 oz. triple sec
3 dashes of bitters
Dash of grenadine

Pour first six ingredients into a glass with ice. Shake. Strain into a chilled glass. Fill with ginger ale. Garnish with orange and cherry.

PILOT HOUSE FIZZ

1 oz. Absolut Citron vodka
1 oz. Hiram Walker triple sec
Dash lime juice
Dash orange bitters
Champagne

Mix first four ingredients with ice in a shaker. Strain into a chilled goblet. Fill with champagne.

PINEAPPLE & POMEGRANATE

1½ oz. Cîroc vodka
1½ oz. pomegranate juice
1 oz. pineapple juice

Shake with crushed ice and strain into a cocktail glass. Garnish with a tropical flower.

PINEAPPLE LEMONADE

2 oz. Skyy vodka
2 oz. pineapple juice
Fresh lemonade

PINEAPPLE PIE

2¼ oz. pineapple vodka, chilled
¼ oz. white crème de cacao

Shake with ice and strain into a rocks glass. Garnish with a dollop of whipped cream.

PINEAPPLE UPSIDE-DOWN CAKE-TINI

1½ oz. Three Olives Vanilla vodka
2 oz. pineapple-coconut rum
1½ oz. cream

Shake with ice and strain into a chilled martini glass. Garnish with a slice of pineapple and a cherry.

PINK BABY

2 oz. Skyy vodka
1 oz. cherry liqueur
1 oz. sweet & sour mix

PINK FLOYD

1 oz. vodka
1 oz. sloe gin
½ cup fresh or canned pineapple

Blend until smooth. Top with soda water. Garnish with a pineapple.

PINK HOTEL

2 oz. vodka
½ oz. crème de noyaux

Shake with ice and strain into a short glass. Add a dash of ginger ale and fill with beer.

PINK LEMONADE

2 oz. Three Olives vodka
1 oz. cranberry juice
½ oz. sour mix

Shake with ice and strain into a chilled martini glass. Garnish with a lime wedge.

PINK LEMONADE II

2 oz. vodka
1 oz. cranberry juice
1¼ oz. sweet & sour mix
½ tsp. sugar
Soda
1 lime wedge

Pour first three ingredients into a tall 12 oz. glass. Stir to dissolve sugar. Add ice and top with soda. Add squeeze of lime from wedge and garnish with remaining wedge.

PINK MINK

1¾ oz. vodka
¼ oz. Bacardi rum
¼ oz. Hiram Walker strawberry liqueur

Combine with ice in a shaker. Strain into a cocktail glass with rim moistened with strawberry liqueur and sugar frosted. Garnish with half a strawberry.

PINK MUSTANG

1 part cranberry vodka, chilled
1 part Rumplemintz peppermint schnapps

Serve on the rocks.

PINK PASSION

2 oz. Three Olives vodka
1 oz. raspberry liqueur
½ oz. sour mix
½ oz. 7 Up

Shake with ice and strain into a chilled martini glass. Garnish with an edible passion flower.

PINK PUSSY CAT

2 oz. Skyy vodka
1 oz. pineapple or grapefruit juice
Dash of grenadine

PINK SQUIRREL

1 part UV vodka
2 parts lemonade
Dash of grenadine

Shake with ice and strain into a martini glass.

PLENTY GOOD

¾ oz. Smirnoff black cherry vodka
¾ oz. Romana sambuca

Pour into a shot glass, chill, and serve.

POMEGRANATE

1½ parts Vox vodka
1 pomegranate/fresh pomegranate juice
Dash of simple syrup

Garnish with one white orchid.

PORCH CLIMBER

1 oz. cherry vodka
½ oz. apricot brandy
½ oz. cherry brandy
Sour mix

Pour first three ingredients into a glass and shake. Fill with sour mix.

PRAIRIE OYSTER

2 oz. vodka
2 oz. tomato juice
Dash Worcestershire sauce

Drop an unbroken egg yolk in the bottom of a chilled wine glass. In a separate mixing glass, combine the other ingredients; mix well. Pour over egg yolk. Salt and pepper to taste.

PREMIER

1½ oz. Skyy vodka
1 oz. raspberry liqueur
Fresh lemon juice

PROUD MARY

2 oz. Skyy vodka
1 oz. Midori melon liqueur
½ oz. triple sec
Pineapple juice
Sweet & sour mix

Pour first three ingredients into a glass and top with pineapple juice, then add a dash of sweet & sour.

PUCKER UP

1 part UV Citruv vodka
2 parts tonic

Serve over ice in a lowball glass.

PURPLE HAZE MARTINI

2 oz. Three Olives Grape vodka
1 oz. raspberry liqueur
Splash of fresh lime juice

Pour raspberry liqueur in bottom of chilled martini glass. Fill with vodka, then add a splash of lime juice.

PURPLE HOOTER

1½ oz. vodka
½ oz. black raspberry liqueur
½ oz. cranberry juice
Splash of club soda

Shake first three ingredients and strain into a glass. Top with a splash of club soda.

PURPLE PASSION

2 oz. Skyy citrus vodka
Grapefruit juice
Grape juice

Pour vodka into a glass and fill with equal parts grapefruit juice and grape juice.

PURPLE RAIN

½ oz. vodka
½ oz. gin
½ oz. rum
½ oz. tequila
½ oz. triple sec
Sour mix
Blackberry liqueur

Pour first five ingredients into a glass with ice and fill with sour mix. Shake. Top with blackberry liqueur and garnish with a lime.

PURPLE-TINI

2 oz. Three Olives Grape vodka
1 oz. triple sec
Splash of raspberry liqueur

Shake with ice and strain into a chilled martini glass. Garnish with an orange slice.

RAINBOW

2 oz. Absolut Citron vodka
Grapefruit juice

Pour vodka into a tall glass over ice and fill with half grapefruit and half grape juice.

RAINBOW II

Equal parts:
Grenadine
Green crème de menthe
Smirnoff vodka
Lime juice

Mix each ingredient with crushed ice and layer into glass.

RASMOPOLITAN

1¼ parts Vox raspberry vodka
½ part Cointreau
1 part cranberry juice
Squeeze of fresh lime

Mix in a shaker half-filled with ice. Pour into a chilled martini glass. Garnish with a lemon peel.

RASPBERRY BURST

1 oz. Smirnoff raspberry vodka
¾ oz. peach schnapps
¼ oz. cranberry juice

Shake with ice and strain into a shot glass.

RASPBERRY COOLER

2 oz. Smirnoff raspberry vodka
3 oz. lemon-lime soda
Splash of fresh squeezed lime juice

Pour into a glass over ice and garnish with a slice of lime.

RASPBERRY KISS

1½ oz. Skyy berry vodka
1 oz. raspberry liqueur
½ oz. white crème de cacao
(optional—splash of half-and-half)

RASPBERRY LEMONADE

2 oz. Smirnoff raspberry vodka
3 oz. lemonade

Pour vodka into a glass over ice and top with lemonade. Garnish with a lemon twist.

RASPBERRY RAIN

1 part Vox raspberry vodka
1 part DeKuyper Pucker raspberry schnapps
1 part DeKuyper Peachtree schnapps
Splash of 7 Up

Mix in a shaker half-filled with ice and pour or strain into a glass.

RASPBERRY SUNRISE

1 part Vox raspberry vodka
½ part Chambord
1 part champagne (float)

Mix vodka and Chambord in a shaker half-filled with ice.

RASPBERRY TRUFFLE MARTINI

1½ parts Vox raspberry vodka
1 part white crème de cacao
¾ part cream
½ part Chambord

Mix in a shaker half-filled with ice. Pour into a cocoa-rimmed martini glass. Garnish with raspberries and a maraschino cherry.

RASPBERRY VODKA & SODA

2½ oz. Smirnoff raspberry vodka

Pour into a glass over ice, stir, and garnish with a lime wedge.

RAZZED UP

1 part Stoli Razberi
3 parts lemon-lime soda
Squeeze of lime

Shake with ice and strain into a chilled cocktail glass.

RAZZLE DAPPLE

1 part Vox green apple vodka
1 part Vox raspberry vodka
Sprite

Pour first two ingredients into a glass and fill with Sprite.

RAZZ-MA-TAZZ

2 oz. vodka, chilled
½ oz. Chambord
1½ oz. club soda

RAZZPUTIN

1 part Vox raspberry vodka
1 part Blue Island Pucker
1 part lemonade
Splash of blue curacao
Splash of Sprite

Shake and pour or strain into a glass. Garnish with raspberries.

RED

2 oz. Skyy vodka
1 oz. Campari

RED APPLE

2 oz. Smirnoff green apple vodka
3 oz. cranberry juice

Pour into a glass over ice and stir well.

RED EYE MARTINI

1 part UV Cherry vodka
2 parts champagne

Stir and pour into a martini glass.

RED PANTIES

1½ oz. peach vodka
½ oz. peach schnapps
Dash of grenadine
1 oz. orange juice
1 oz. cranberry juice

Shake and strain into a chilled glass.

RED ROOSTER

1½ oz. Skyy vodka
1 oz. sloe gin
3 oz. orange or grapefruit juice
1½ oz. seltzer water
½ tsp. Frank's Redhot Cayenne Pepper Sauce

RED ZIPPER

1 oz. vodka
1 oz. Galliano
Cranberry juice

Pour first two ingredients into a glass with ice and fill with cranberry juice. Stir and garnish with a lime.

RICKEY

2 oz. Skyy vodka
Juice of one lime
Club soda

Pour first two ingredients into a glass and fill with club soda.

ROBITUSSIN

1 oz. Three Olives cherry vodka
1 oz. root beer schnapps

Pour into a shot glass and serve.

ROCKET CLASSIC

2 oz. Three Olives vodka
4 oz. club soda
Splash of cranberry juice

Mix first two ingredients in a glass over ice. Add a big splash of cranberry juice and garnish with a lemon or lime wedge.

ROCKS

2 parts Vox vodka
4 parts tonic water or soda

Build over ice in a rocks glass. Garnish with a slice of lemon, a slice of lime, and a slice of kumquat.

ROCKY ROAD

1 oz. Three Olives vodka
½ oz. coconut-flavored rum
½ oz. Disaronno amaretto
½ oz. crème de cacao

Shake over ice and strain into a chilled martini glass. Garnish with a cherry.

ROOT BEER FLOATINI

1½ oz. Skyy vanilla vodka
1½ oz. root beer schnapps

ROYAL WASHINGTON APPLE

1 oz. Crown Royal
¼ oz. Smirnoff green apple vodka

Shake with ice and pour into a glass.

ROYALE DE FRANCE MARTINI

2 oz. Three Olives vodka
¼ oz. peach schnapps
¼ oz. Chambord
½ oz. white peach puree
¼ oz. chilled champagne

Shake first four ingredients with ice and strain into a chilled martini glass. Top with champagne.

RUBY CITRUS

2 oz. Skyy citrus vodka
1 oz. ruby red grapefruit juice

RUBY RED MARTINI

3 oz. Three Olives vodka
Splash of triple sec
1 oz. red grapefruit juice

Shake with ice and strain into a chilled martini glass. Garnish with an orange wedge.

RUBY SLIPPERS

1 part cranberry vodka, chilled
1 part Goldschlager

Shake and serve on the rocks.

RUDOLPH THE RUBY-TINI

2 oz. Skyy vodka
2 oz. ruby red grapefruit juice

RUMPLE MY VODKA SHOT

1 oz. Three Olives vodka
½ oz. peppermint schnapps

Shake with ice and strain into a shot glass.

RUSSIAN BABE

2 oz. Skyy vodka
½ oz. coffee liqueur
½ oz. Chambord

Shake. Pour over ice or serve straight up.

RUSSIAN KNIGHT

1 oz. Kremlyovskaya
½ oz. Kahlua
½ oz. cream or milk

Shake and stir.

RUSSIAN MONK

2 oz. vodka
1 oz. Frangelico
½ oz. heavy cream

Add ice, shake, and strain into glass.

SAKETINI

2 oz. Skyy vodka
1 oz. sake
Dash of Cinzano dry vermouth

SALT AND PEPPAR

2 oz. Absolut Peppar vodka

Pour chilled vodka into a salt-rimmed cocktail glass. Garnish with a cucumber spear.

SALT LICK

1¼ oz. Sobieski vodka
2 oz. bitter lemon soda
2 oz. grapefruit juice

Pour over ice in a salt-rimmed glass with ice.

SALTY DOG

1 oz. Smirnoff Red Label vodka
1 oz. grapefruit juice

Stir in a shaker and serve over ice in a salt-rimmed glass.

SCREAMING GRASSHOPPER

1 oz. Skyy vodka
1 oz. green crème de menthe
1 oz. white crème de cacao
Splash of heavy cream

SCREWDRIVER

2 oz. vodka
Orange juice

Pour the vodka into a glass and fill with orange juice.

SEABREEZE

2 oz. Sobieski vodka
Cranberry juice
Grapefruit juice

Pour vodka over ice into a tall glass. Fill halfway with grapefruit juice and top off with cranberry juice.

SEASONS GREETINGS

2 oz. Skyy vodka
½ oz. Skyy citrus vodka
½ oz. green crème de menthe

SZECHUAN SURPRISE

2 oz. Amaretto
1 oz. Yazi
4 splashes of peach bitters

SERIAL LOVER

1½ oz. Skyy vodka
½ oz. coconut rum
½ oz. spiced rum
Pineapple juice

Pour first three ingredients into a glass and fill with pineapple juice.

SEX IN THE CITRUS

2 oz. Skyy citrus vodka
1 oz. peach schnapps
Cranberry juice
Orange juice

Pour first two ingredients into a glass and fill with equal parts of cranberry juice and orange juice.

SEX IN THE CITY

2 oz. Skyy vodka
1 oz. peach schnapps

SEXY MELON

2 oz. Skyy vodka
1 oz. Midori melon liqueur
1 oz. raspberry liqueur
Orange juice or pineapple juice
Cranberry juice

Pour first three ingredients into a glass and fill with equal parts orange juice or pineapple juice and cranberry juice.

SEX ON THE BEACH

1 oz. vodka
1 oz. Midori
1 oz. pineapple juice
1 oz. cranberry juice

Build in a mixing glass, shake or stir, and strain into a 5 oz. glass.

SHANGHAI LEMON DROP

2 oz. lemoncello
1 oz. Yazi
4 splashes of peach bitters

SHARK

1 oz. Skyy vodka
1 oz. 1800 tequila
Dash of Tabasco sauce

Serve on the rocks or as a shot.

SIBERIAN SUNRISE

2 oz. Skyy vodka
3 oz. grapefruit juice
1 oz. Cointreau

Serve in a tall glass.

SILVER BULLET

1 oz. vodka
½ oz. peppermint schnapps
Serve in a shot glass.

SLIDE

2 oz. Skyy vodka
1 oz. hazelnut liqueur
1 oz. Carolans Irish cream
Splash of milk

SLIM JIM

2 oz. vodka
Diet soda

Pour vodka into a highball glass with ice and fill with diet soda. Garnish with a lemon or lime slice.

SMIRNOFF AND PAPAYA

1½ oz. Smirnoff vodka
6 oz. papaya nectar
½ oz. triple sec
1 tsp. fresh lime juice

Pour into a tall glass over ice. Garnish with fresh sliced papaya.

SMIRNOFF LIME ICE

2 oz. Smirnoff lime vodka
1 large scoop lime sherbet
Coarsely grated lime rind

In a stemmed glass, pour vodka over sherbet. Sprinkle with lime rind.

SMIRNOFF ORANGE SPARKLER

2 oz. Smirnoff orange vodka
5 oz. tonic water

Pour into a glass over ice. Garnish with an orange twist.

SMIRNOFF VANILLA COLA

2 oz. vanilla Smirnoff vanilla vodka
6 oz. Canada Dry Jamaica cola

Pour into a tall glass over ice. Garnish with a wedge of lime.

SMIRNOFF VANILLA GINGER

2 oz. Smirnoff vanilla vodka
Splash ginger ale

In a rocks glass, over shaved ice, pour vodka. Add a splash of ginger ale.

SMOKY MARTINI

1¼ oz. vodka
Dash Glenlivet single malt scotch

Pour over ice. Shake or stir well. Strain and serve in a cocktail glass straight up or over ice. Garnish with a twist.

SNOWDRIFT MARTINI

2 oz. Skyy vanilla vodka
1 oz. amaretto
4 oz. sweet & sour mix

SNOWFLAKE

1 oz. Skyy vodka
1 oz. crème de cacao
1 oz. Frangelico
2 oz. cream or milk

Serve straight up in a chilled martini glass.

S.O.S.

1 part Ohranj vodka
1 part sambuca

Serve on the rocks.

SOVIET COCKTAIL

1½ oz. vodka
½ oz. dry vermouth
½ oz. dry sherry
Lemon peel

Mix all ingredients, except lemon peel, with cracked ice in a shaker or blender and strain into a chilled cocktail glass. Twist lemon peel over drink and drop into glass.

SPA MARTINI

2 oz. Skyy vodka
Fresh cucumber
Fresh mint
Splash of simple syrup

SPICY CITRI-POLITAN

2 oz. Skyy citrus vodka
1 oz. Cointreau
1 oz. pink grapefruit juice
½ tsp. super fine sugar
¼ tsp. Frank's Redhot Chile 'n Lime Hot Sauce

SPICY HAMILTON

2 oz. Skyy vodka
½ oz. Cinzano dry vermouth
3 drops Tabasco sauce

SPLASH

2 oz. Skyy vodka
Dash of lime juice
Splash of blue curacao
Splash of sweet & sour
1 oz. champagne

SPOTTED DOG

¼ oz. vodka
¾ oz. Hiram Walker amaretto
¼ oz. Hiram Walker white crème de cacao
Vanilla ice cream

Mix all ingredients in a blender until smooth. Pour into cocktail glass and serve.

SPRING MARTINI

3 oz. Teton Glacier potato vodka
2 tbsp. fresh lime juice
1 tbsp. crème de cassis

Shake. Serve in a chilled martini glass.

ST. PETERSBURG

2 oz. vodka
¼ tsp. orange bitters
1 orange wedge

Mix first two ingredients over several ice cubes. Stir until very cold and pour into a chilled old-fashioned glass. Score peel of orange wedge with tines of fork and drop into drink.

STAR ANISE

1 part Vox vodka
Dry vermouth
2 anise stars (dried ripe fruit anise)

Infuse the anise stars in 3 oz. dry vermouth overnight. Taint the ice in a mixing glass by adding a splash of vermouth. Add vodka and stir.

STARLIGHT ROOM MARTINI

2 oz. Skyy vodka
½ oz. passion fruit liqueur
½ oz. Campari
Dash of fresh lemon juice

STOLAR SUN

2 oz. Stoli
2 oz. orange juice
½ oz. grenadine

Pour first two ingredients into a rocks glass over ice. Slowly pour in grenadine.

STRAIGHT-UP MARTINI

3 oz. Skyy vodka
2 olives

Shake with ice. Serve in a chilled martini glass.

STRASBERI SHORTCAKE

1 oz. Stolichnaya Strasberi vodka
1 oz. Stolichnaya Vanil vodka

Pour all ingredients over ice in a large mixing glass or cocktail shaker. Stir and strain into a chilled martini glass. Garnish with a strawberry slice.

STRAWBERRY ANTIFREEZE

1 part UV Apple vodka
2 strawberries

Blend with ice and serve in a tropical glass.

STRAWBERRY SHORTCAKE

1½ oz. Skyy Vanilla vodka
2 oz. cranberry juice
Splash of cream
Dash of grenadine

Shake with ice. Serve straight up in a martini glass.

STRAWBERRY SUNRISE

2 oz. Smirnoff strawberry vodka
2 oz. orange juice
½ oz. grenadine or cranberry juice

Pour into a glass over ice and stir well. Garnish with a strawberry.

SUMMER VODKA MOJITO CLASSIC

2 oz. Three Olives vodka
3 slices of lime
3–4 mint leaves
1 tbsp. sugar
4 oz. soda water

Muddle vodka, lime, mint and sugar in a tall glass. Fill with ice and pour soda water to top.

SUMO SLAM

Equal parts:
Vox vodka
DeKuyper Pucker sour apple schnapps
Splash of sake

Serve as a shot.

SUNBURN

2 oz. Smirnoff vodka
1 oz. Arrow cranberry schnapps
3 oz. orange juice

Pour first two ingredients into a tall glass over ice. Over back of spoon, pour in cranberry schnapps. Garnish with an orange.

SUNBURST

2 oz. Absolut vodka
Dash triple sec
Grapefruit juice

Serve in a rocks glass over ice. Add a dash of triple sec.

SUNNY

2 oz. Skyy citrus vodka
½ oz. triple sec
Lemonade

Pour first two ingredients into a glass and fill with lemonade.

SUNRISE MARTINI

2 oz. Skyy vodka
1 oz. 1800 tequila
Splash of Grand Marnier
Splash of grenadine

SUNSET

2 oz. Skyy vodka
2 oz. grapefruit juice
2 dashes of grenadine
Twist of lime peel

SUNSHINE FROSTY PUNCH

2 oz. vodka
2 scoops vanilla ice cream

Blend until smooth and serve in a 12 oz. brandy snifter.

SUNSTROKE

2 oz. Sobieski vodka
3 oz. grapefruit juice
Splash of Cointreau

Pour first two ingredients into a short glass over ice. Top with triple sec and stir. Sugar may be substituted for triple sec.

SURFER'S SUNRISE TROPICAL

1½ oz. Three Olives vodka
1½ oz. orange juice
1½ oz. pineapple juice
Splash of grenadine

Mix first three ingredients in a glass over ice. Top with a splash of grenadine. Garnish with a cherry.

SWEDISH BEAR

¾ oz. Absolut vodka
½ oz. Godiva
1 tbsp. heavy cream

Pour over ice in a chilled old fashioned glass, and stir.

SWEDISH COCKTAIL

¾ oz. Absolut vodka
¼ oz. Beefeater gin
¼ oz. Hiram Walker white crème de cacao

Shake with ice and strain into a chilled cocktail glass.

SWEDISH LADY

1 oz. Absolut vodka
¼ oz. Hiram Walker strawberry liqueur
1 oz. lemon juice
1 oz. sugar syrup
½ oz. heavy cream

Combine in a shaker with ice. Strain into a chilled whiskey sour glass.

SWEET MARIA

2 oz. Skyy vodka
1 tbsp. light cream
½ oz. amaretto

TABOO

1½ oz. pineapple vodka, chilled
½ oz. cranberry juice
½ oz. sour mix
Splash of triple sec

Blend with crushed ice and serve in a tall glass. Garnish with a pineapple wedge and a cherry.

TANGERINE

1¼ oz. Ohranj vodka
2 oz. orange juice
Dash of grenadine

Shake with ice and pour or strain into a glass.

TAXI

1 part Ohranj vodka
1 part coffee liqueur

Serve on the rocks.

TEN BLUE LAGOON

1 oz. Tanqueray No. Ten
¼ oz. Smirnoff Red Label vodka
¼ oz. blue curacao
Splash of lime juice

Build over ice in a highball glass.

TESTAROSSA

1 oz. vodka
½ oz. Campari
Tonic

*Pour first two ingredients into a tall glass over ice. Top with tonic.
Garnish with a slice of lemon and a slice of lime.*

TEQUILA PAIN KILLER

1 oz. Jose Cuervo Especial tequila
½ oz. Smirnoff Red Label vodka
½ oz. light rum
2 oz. pineapple juice
1 oz. orange juice
½ oz. cream of coconut

Blend until smooth and pour into a glass with ice. Garnish with a pineapple slice.

THE SNUGGLER HOT

½ oz. Three Olives vodka
¾ oz. peppermint schnapps
¾ oz. Kahlua
6 oz. hot chocolate

Mix in a glass mug. Top with whipped cream and chocolate sauce.

THE THRILLER WITH VANILLA

2 oz. Kremlyovskaya chocolate vodka
¼ oz. vanilla extract
Half-and-half

Blend until smooth and pour into a glass.

THE TRIPLE SOUTH

3 oz. Three Olives vodka
1 oz. tequila

Shake tequila with ice until coated. Strain and discard tequila. Keep ice in the shaker. Add vodka to the same shaker and shake. Strain into a chilled martini glass and garnish with jalapenos or olives.

THE TWIST

1 oz. vodka
½ oz. Hiram Walker white crème de menthe
Orange sherbet

Blend. Pour into a champagne glass.

THE ULTIMATE CITRUS MARTINI

2 oz. Three Olives citrus vodka
½ oz. grapefruit juice
½ oz. pineapple juice
Splash of triple sec

Shake with ice and strain into a chilled martini glass.

TRANSFUSION

2 oz. Sobieski vodka
Grape juice

Pour vodka into a tall glass with ice and fill with grape juice. Top with club soda.

UV LEMON BOMB

1 part UV Lemonade vodka
8 oz. can of energy drink

UV PINK FLAMINGO

2 parts UV Lemonade vodka
1 part cranberry juice
Splash of triple sec

UV SHANDY

1½ oz. UV Lemonade vodka
12 oz. light beer

UV ULTIMATE LEMONADE

2 parts UV Lemonade vodka
2 parts lemonade
A splash of sparkling water

Shake with ice and strain into a martini glass.

THE VOX RASPBERRY POMEGRANATE

1 part Vox raspberry vodka
2 parts Pom Wonderful pomegranate juice
Splash of triple sec
Splash of simple syrup or 7 Up

Shake well and strain into a chilled martini glass.

TIME MACHINE

2 oz. Skyy vodka
1 oz. amaretto
Orange juice

Pour first two ingredients into a glass and fill with orange juice.

TINSEL TINI

1 oz. Cîroc vodka
½ oz. Rumplemintz
¼ oz. Godiva white chocolate liqueur

Shake with ice and strain into a martini glass.

TIRAMISU

1 oz. Skyy vodka
1 oz. Vermeer chocolate cream liqueur
1 oz. Kahlua

TITANIC MARTINI

3 oz. Teton Glacier potato vodka
Vermouth to taste

Stir only. No shaking.

TKO

1 oz. Kremlyovskaya chocolate vodka
¾ oz. Rumplemintz
¼ oz. crème de cacao light

Shake and strain into a glass.

TONGUE TEASER

2 oz. Smirnoff orange vodka
1 oz. lemonade
2 oz. cranberry juice

Build over ice and stir well.

TRICK OR PEACH

1½ oz. Skyy berry vodka
½ oz. peach liqueur
Splash of sour mix

Build on ice and stir well.

TROPICAL CITRUS MARTINI

1 oz. Skyy citrus vodka
1 oz. coconut rum
½ oz. pineapple juice
½ oz. orange juice

Shake. Serve over ice.

TROPICAL ICEBERG

1½ oz. pineapple vodka, chilled
½ oz. banana liqueur or ½ banana
½ oz. cream of coconut
Dash of cream or half-and-half

Shake or blend.

TROPICAL SCREW

2 oz. Skyy vodka
½ oz. triple sec
Orange juice

Pour first two ingredients into a glass and fill with orange juice.

TROPICAL SLEIGH RIDE

½ oz. Skyy citrus vodka
½ oz. DeKuyper Peachtree schnapps
½ oz. triple sec
1 oz. sweet & sour mix
1 oz. pineapple juice
Splash of grenadine

Shake with ice.

TUXEDO MARTINI

1 oz. Kremlyovskaya vodka
¾ oz. Stolichnaya vanilla vodka

Serve over ice.

TWISTED FRUIT

2 oz. Three Olives grape vodka
½ oz. triple sec
2 oz. grapefruit juice

Shake with ice and strain into a chilled martini glass. Garnish with a lime wedge.

ULTIMATE MARTINI

3 oz. Skyy vodka, chilled
Hint of Cinzano extra-dry vermouth

Shake or stir. Serve up or on the rocks.

UV MARTINI

2½ oz. UV vodka

Shake with ice and strain into a martini glass.

VANILLATINI

2 oz. Skyy vanilla vodka
Splash of lemon-lime soda

Serve in a tall glass with ice.

VANILLA AND COLA

2 oz. Skyy vanilla vodka
Cola

Pour vodka into a glass and fill with cola.

VANILLA APPLETINI

1½ oz. Skyy vanilla vodka
1 oz. sour apple liqueur
Splash of lemon-lime soda

Serve over ice.

VANILLA BANSHEE

2 oz. Skyy vanilla vodka
1 oz. banana liqueur
½ oz. white crème de cacao
Splash of cream

Shake or blend.

VANILLA CRUSH

1½ oz. Smirnoff vanilla vodka
3 oz. lemon-lime soda
Splash of orange juice

Pour into a glass over ice and stir well.

VANILLA ICED TEA

1 part UV Vanilla vodka
1 part tequila
1 part rum
1 part gin
1 part cola
2 parts lemon juice

Serve over ice in a highball glass.

VANILLA MALTED

3 parts Absolut vanilla vodka
2 parts cream liqueur
1 part hazelnut liqueur
1 part cream

Shake with ice and strain into a martini glass. Top with shaved white chocolate.

VANILLA RAIN

2 oz. Smirnoff vanilla vodka
3 oz. lemon-lime soda

Pour into a glass over ice and stir well. Garnish with a lime twist.

VANILLA SODA

2 oz. Skyy vanilla vodka
Root beer

Pour vodka into a glass and fill with root beer.

VANILLA VIXEN

1 oz. Skyy vanilla vodka
2 oz. Skyy citrus vodka
1 oz. Midori melon liqueur
½ oz. lime juice

Shake with ice. Serve over the rocks.

VANILLA VODKA & SODA

2 oz. Smirnoff vanilla vodka
4 oz. soda

Pour into a glass over ice and stir well. Garnish with a slice of lime.

VANILLA AND GINGER

2 oz. Skyy vanilla vodka
Ginger ale

Pour vodka into a glass and fill with ginger ale.

VELVET ANGEL

2 oz. Vodka 02
¼ oz. chambord
⅛ oz. triple sec
⅛ oz. raspberry puree
Cranberry juice

Pour first four ingredients into a glass and top with cranberry juice.
Shake and serve over ice in a 14 oz. glass. Garnish with raspberries.

VENUS

2 oz. Skyy vodka
½ oz. tart lemonade
½ oz. passion fruit liqueur

Serve in a tall glass.

VINE WINE

1½ parts Vox vodka
1 part of pinot noir
Dash of simple syrup
1 bunch of small red grapes

Muddle six red grapes in a mixing glass. Add the wine, simple syrup and Vox vodka.

VODKA BLUE OCEAN

1 oz. Cîroc vodka
½ oz. blue curacao
¾ oz. grapefruit juice
Splash of sugar

Shake with crushed ice and strain into a cocktail glass. Garnish with a white orchid.

VODKA AND COLA

1½ oz. Smirnoff Red Label vodka
3 oz. cola

Pour into a glass with ice and garnish with a lime wedge.

VODKA ESPRESSO

1 oz. Cîroc vodka
½ oz. Godiva cappuccino liqueur
1 oz. cold espresso
Splash of simple syrup

Pour into a glass over ice and stir. Garnish with three coffee beans.

VODKA FROST GRAPE-TINI

1 oz. Cîroc vodka
¼ oz. Grand Marnier
¼ oz. blue curacao
Splash of red grape juice
1 tbsp. purple grape sugar

Shake first four ingredients with crushed ice and strain into a cocktail glass rimmed with purple grape sugar.

VODKA MULE

1 part Absolut vodka
Dash of lime juice
Ginger beer

Build over ice in a long drink glass. Garnish with lime wedges.

VODKA PASSION

1 oz. Cîroc vodka
½ oz. peach schnapps
½ oz. watermelon pucker
4 oz. lemon-lime soda

Shake with crushed ice and strain into a tall glass. Garnish with an orange slice.

VODKA AND TONIC

2 oz. Sobieski vodka
Tonic

Pour vodka into a tall glass over ice and fill with tonic. Add a squeeze of lime.

VODKA ROYAL COSMOPOLITAN

1 oz. Cîroc vodka
½ oz. champagne
1 oz. cranberry juice
Splash of triple sec
Splash of lime juice

Garnish with an orange twist.

VODKA SANGRIA (SERVES EIGHT)

1 bottle rosé wine
6 oz. Cîroc vodka
3 oz. Grand Marnier
2 oz. white grape juice
2 oz. lemon juice
2 oz. simple syrup
3 oz. pomegranate juice
3 oz. strained orange juice
1 bottle club soda
1 box blackberries or raspberries (for garnish)

Pour first eight ingredients into a large pitcher half filled with ice (entire mixture should be light pink). Pour in glasses over small amount of fresh ice and top each with about ½ oz. of club soda. Garnish with blackberries or raspberries.

VODKA ULTIMATE GRAPE

¾ oz. Cîroc vodka
¾ oz. champagne
¾ oz. fresh white grape juice

Shake with ice and strain into a martini glass.

VODKA WASABI MARTINI

1½ oz. Cîroc vodka
Dash of wasabi
Splash of lemon juice
Splash of sugar syrup

Shake with ice and strain into a martini glass. Garnish with one round pea.

VOODOO SHOT

¾ oz. Skyy vodka, chilled
¾ oz. peppermint schnapps, chilled

Serve in a shot glass.

WATERMELON

1 oz. vodka
1 oz. honeydew melon liqueur
2 oz. orange juice
2 oz. cranberry juice

Pour into a glass over ice and fill with equal parts orange and cranberry juices.

WATERMELON DROP

1½ oz. Smirnoff watermelon vodka
3 oz. energy drink

Pour into a glass over ice and stir well.

WATERMELON MARTINI

3 oz. Teton Glacier potato vodka
3 oz. watermelon, pureed in blender

Pour into a glass and garnish with a small slice of watermelon.

WATERMELON MARTINI

2 oz. Skyy vodka
Fresh watermelon cubes (1 inch by 1 inch)
1 oz. Midori melon liqueur
½ oz. orange liqueur or triple sec
Splash of sweet & sour mix

WATERMELON SPLASH

1½ oz. Smirnoff watermelon vodka
3 oz. lemon-lime soda
Splash of cranberry juice

Pour into a glass over ice and stir well. Garnish with a watermelon slice.

WATERMELONTINI

1½ oz. Three Olives watermelon vodka
1½ oz. Three Olives citrus vodka
1½ oz. cranberry juice

Shake with ice and strain into a chilled martini glass. Garnish with a cherry.

WHISPER MARTINI

2½ ounces Teton Glacier potato vodka
1 or 2 drops dry vermouth

Garnish to taste, quietly, with a potato slice.

WHITE CHOCOLATE MARTINI

2 oz. Skyy vodka
¼ oz. white chocolate liqueur

Shake. Serve straight up or on the rocks.

WHITE CHRISTMAS

2 oz. Skyy vodka
1 oz. crème de menthe, white

Garnish with candy cane.

WHITE CHRISTMAS COSMO

1½ oz. Skyy citrus vodka
½ oz. triple sec
Squeeze of fresh lime
Splash of white cranberry juice

Shake with ice. Serve on the rocks.

WHITE ELEPHANT

2 oz. vodka
¼ oz. crème de cacao
Milk

Serve in a tall glass with ice.

WHITE KNUCKLES

Equal parts:
Kremlyovskaya
Baileys Irish cream

Shake with ice and strain into a glass.

WHITE MONK

3 oz. Skyy vanilla vodka
1 oz. Frangelico
Splash of cream

WHITE RUSSIAN

2 oz. Skyy vodka
1 oz. coffee liqueur
Cream

Pour into a glass and top with cream.

WHITE RUSSIAN II

1 oz. vodka
½ oz. Godiva liqueur
½ oz. heavy cream

Shake and pour into a rocks glass over ice.

WHITE SPIDER

2 parts Absolut vodka
1 part white crème de menthe

Stir on the rocks.

WINTER

1½ oz. Skyy orange vodka
½ oz. blue curacao
1 oz. champagne

Serve in a champagne glass.

WINTER SOLSTICE

2 oz. Skyy citrus vodka
½ oz. fresh lemon juice
¼ oz. fresh pomegranate juice
1 oz. simple syrup

Shake with ice. Serve over ice.

WINTER SPARKLER

1 part Vox raspberry vodka
½ part chambord liqueur
½ part sour mix
½ part cranberry juice
Champagne float

Shake over ice and pour or strain into a glass.

WINTER WHITE COSMO

2 oz. Skyy citrus vodka
½ oz. triple sec
Squeeze of fresh lime
Splash of white cranberry juice

Shake over ice and pour or strain into a glass.

WOO WOO

2 oz. Skyy vodka
1 oz. peach schnapps
Splash of cranberry juice

Shake over ice and pour or strain into a glass.

X-RAY

1 part UV Vanilla vodka
3 parts cola

Serve over ice in a highball glass.

YAZI APPLE BLOSSOM

1 oz. of Yazi ginger vodka
5 oz. apple juice (unfiltered juice will produce a darker cocktail;
   sparkling apple juice adds pretty bubbles)
½ oz. amaretto

Serve in a tall glass.

YELLOW FEVER

2 oz. Smirnoff vodka
5 oz. grapefruit juice

Pour into a large goblet over ice. Garnish with a twist of lemon.

50
FOOD RECIPES USING VODKA

HARVEY WALLBANGER CAKE

HARVEY WALLBANGER GLAZE

For cake:
2 tbsp. Three Olives vodka
Vegetable oil spray (for misting the pan)
Flour (for dusting the pan)
1 package (18.25 oz.) plain orange cake mix
1 package (3.4 oz.) vanilla instant pudding mix
4 large eggs
½ cup vegetable oil
½ cup fresh orange juice (from 2 to 3 oranges)
½ cup Galliano

For glaze:
1 tsp. Three Olives vodka
1 cup confectioner's sugar, sifted
1 tbsp. orange juice
1 tbsp. Galliano

Place a rack in the center of the oven and preheat the oven to 350° F. Lightly mist a 12-cup bundt pan with vegetable oil spray, then dust with flour. Shake out the excess flour. Set the pan aside.

Place the cake mix, pudding mix, eggs, oil, orange juice, Galliano, and vodka in a large mixing bowl. Blend with an electric mixer on low speed for 1 minute. Stop the machine and scrape down the sides of the bowl with a rubber spatula. Increase the mixer speed to medium, and beat 2 minutes more, scraping down the sides again if needed. The batter should look thick and smooth. Pour the batter into the prepared pan, smoothing it out with the rubber spatula. Place the pan in the oven.

Bake the cake for 45 to 50 minutes, until it is golden brown and springs back when touched. Remove the pan from the oven and place it on a wire rack to cool for 20 minutes. Run a long, sharp knife around the edge of the cake and invert it on a serving platter. Poke holes in the top of the cake with a wooden skewer or toothpick.

Prepare the glaze. Place the confectioners sugar, orange juice, Galliano, and vodka in a small bowl and stir until smooth. Spoon the glaze over the warm cake, allowing it to seep into the holes and drizzle down the sides and into the center. Allow the cake to cool completely before slicing.

Baked cake can be stored covered in aluminum foil or plastic wrap at room temperature for up to 4 days. Or freeze it, wrapped in foil, and store for up to 6 months. Thaw the cake overnight on the counter before serving. Serves 16.

BLACK RUSSIAN CAKE

¼ cup Three Olives vodka
1 package yellow cake mix
1 package chocolate instant pudding mix (4 ½ oz.)
1 cup oil
4 eggs
¼ cup Kahlua
¾ cup water
½ cup confectioners sugar
Additional Kahlua

Combine cake mix, pudding mix, oil, eggs, vodka, Kahlua, and water and beat 4 minutes. Turn into a greased and floured bundt pan.

Bake at 350° F for 50 minutes. Cool for ½ hour and then remove from pan and glaze with confectioners sugar, moistened with additional Kahlua liqueur.

STRAWBERRY VODKA SAUCE

2 ounces Three Olives vodka
2 tbsp. unsalted butter
¼ cup white sugar
2 cups sliced fresh strawberries

Melt butter in a small skillet over medium heat. Stir in the sugar until dissolved, then add strawberries. Cook, stirring occasionally, until the strawberries are hot. Pour the vodka over the berries, and carefully light. Let the flames burn off, then remove pan from the heat.

LEMON MADELEINES WITH LEMON VODKA SYRUP

For Madeleines:
2 cups cake flour (not self-rising)
1 tsp. baking powder
½ tsp. salt
3 tbsp. plus 1 tsp. freshly grated lemon zest (from about 7 large lemons)
1 cup (2 sticks) unsalted butter, softened
2 tsp. fresh lemon juice
2 cups sugar
6 large eggs

For lemon syrup:
¼ cup Three Olives citrus vodka
¼ cup water
¼ cup sugar
¼ cup fresh lemon juice

To make Madeleines:

Preheat oven to 325° F. Butter and flour a Madeleine pan (preferably nonstick), knocking out excess flour.

In a bowl, sift the flour, baking powder, salt, and lemon zest together.

In another bowl, beat together butter, lemon juice, and sugar with an electric mixer, until mixture is light and fluffy. Add the lemon zest. Beat in eggs, 1 at a time, beating well after each addition. Then add flour mixture, beating until just combined.

Spoon some of the batter into prepared Madeleine molds, filling each mold ¾ full. Using both hands, pick up the Madeleine tray and lightly tap against the table to spread the batter evenly. This will eliminate any air pockets and ensure that molds are not overfilled.

Bake Madeleines in the middle of the oven for 20 to 25 minutes, or until edges are browned and tops are golden. Loosen edges and transfer Madeleines to a rack set over a baking dish. Make more Madeleines in cleaned and freshly buttered and floured pan.

To make lemon syrup:

While first batch of Madeleines is baking, in a small saucepan bring syrup ingredients to a boil, stirring, and remove from heat.

Brush warm Madeleines with some of the hot syrup. Repeat with remaining Madeleines as they are baked, keeping syrup warm.

VODKA LEMON-MERINGUE LAYER CAKE

For lemon sponge cake:
4 large eggs, separated
⅔ cup sugar
1 lemon, zested

½ tsp. vanilla
½ cup all-purpose flour
½ cup cornstarch

For lemon curd:
6 egg yolks
½ cup sugar
½ cup fresh lemon juice
4 oz. (1 stick) unsalted butter, cut into pieces

For citron syrup:
½ cup Three Olives citrus vodka
½ cup sugar

For Meringue icing:
1½ cups sugar
2 tbsp. light corn syrup
⅓ cup cold water
3 egg whites
½ tsp. cream of tartar
Pinch salt
1½ tsp. vanilla extract
1 tbsp. fresh lemon juice
1 tbsp. hot water

To make lemon sponge cake:
Preheat the oven to 350° F. Lightly grease and line the bottom of a 9-inch springform pan with parchment paper and set aside.

In a bowl fitted with an electric mixer, whip the egg yolks, ⅓ cup of the sugar, lemon zest, and vanilla on medium-high speed until thick and almost doubled in volume. (The yolks will form slowly dissolving ribbons when the whip is lifted out.)

In a clean bowl, whip the egg whites on medium speed until frothy. Gradually add the remaining ⅓ cup of sugar, and whip on high speed until stiff peaks form. Fold the egg whites into the egg yolk mixture, being careful not to over mix. Sift half of the flour and cornstarch into the egg mixture, and gently fold to incorporate. Repeat with the remaining flour and cornstarch. Pour the batter into the prepared pan and bake for 20 minutes.

Turn the cake 180°, and bake for an additional 15 to 20 minutes, or until a toothpick comes out clean and the cake starts to pull away from the sides of the pan. Remove from the oven and cool on a wire rack.

To make lemon curd:
In the top of a double boiler, or in a stainless steel bowl, whisk together the yolks, sugar, and lemon juice. Place over simmering water and whisk until thickened. Remove from the heat and whisk in the butter until all is incorporated.

Cover with plastic wrap, pressing down against the surface to prevent a skin from forming. Refrigerate until cool, about 3 hours or overnight.

To make citron syrup:
In a small, heavy saucepan, combine the sugar and vodka. Gently heat, stirring occasionally, until the sugar dissolves.

To assemble the cake:
Slice the cake into 3 layers horizontally. Place the top layer of cake in the bottom of the springform pan and brush with ⅓ of the citron syrup. Spread 1 cup of lemon curd on top and smooth evenly. Repeat with the remaining 2 cake layers, citron syrup and lemon curd. Refrigerate while making the meringue icing.

To make meringue icing:
In a small, heavy saucepan, combine the sugar, corn syrup, and cold water. Bring to a boil, stirring until the sugar dissolves. Boil, uncovered, until the syrup reaches the soft ball stage (240° F) on a candy thermometer. Remove from the heat.

Meanwhile, in a large bowl, beat the egg whites, cream of tartar, and salt with an electric mixer until frothy. With the machine running, slowly pour the syrup down the sides of the bowl into the whites (being careful not to pour the syrup into the moving wire whisk). When all the syrup has been added, add the vanilla and continue beating until the mixture has cooled and is fluffy, for about 3 minutes. Add the lemon juice and water, and set aside.

To assemble the cake, continued:
Remove the cake from the refrigerator and unwrap. Remove the sides of the pan and spread the icing in a thin layer over the sides and top of the cake. Put the remaining icing in a pastry bag fitted with a star tip and decoratively pipe rosettes on top of the cake.

Refrigerate until ready to serve. Prior to serving, with a blowtorch, brown the meringue lightly.

Propane gas torch warning: Propane gas torches are highly flammable and should be kept away from heat or flame, and should not be exposed to prolonged sunlight. Propane gas torches should only be used in well-ventilated areas. When lighting a propane gas torch, place the torch on a flat, steady surface, facing away from you. Light the match or lighter and then open the gas valve. Light the gas jet, and blow out the match. Always turn off the burner valve to "finger tight" when finished using the torch. Children should never use a propane gas torch without adult supervision.

CRANBERRY MOLD

¾ cup Three Olives orange vodka
2¼ cups cranberry juice cocktail
1 box (0.6 oz.) sugar-free cranberry gelatin (recommended brand: Jell-O)
1 (16 oz.) can whole berry cranberry sauce (recommended brand: Ocean Spray)
2 tbsp. orange zest
½ cup chopped pecans
Fresh cranberries and mint sprigs, for garnish

In a medium saucepan, bring the cranberry juice to a boil. Transfer to a medium mixing bowl and pour in the gelatin. Stir until gelatin is completely dissolved. Stir in vodka. Chill 1½ to 2 hours in the refrigerator until it begins to set. Stir in remaining ingredients. Divide into 12 (4 oz.) molds. Refrigerate at least 4 hours to set.

Remove from molds by first running the tip of a sharp knife around the edge of the mold to loosen side. Then dip the bottom of mold in a bowl of warm water. Invert onto a plate. Serve garnished with fresh cranberries and a sprig of fresh mint.

APPLES WITH WARM GOAT CHEESE CROSTINI

2 oz. Three Olives apple vodka
1 baguette
¼ cup olive oil
Salt and freshly ground black pepper
1 tbsp. butter
1 green apple, sliced
1 cup softened goat cheese

Preheat oven on low broil setting.

Slice baguette into 35 small rounds. Coat each round with olive oil and lightly salt and pepper them. Place them on a cookie sheet. In a small saucepan, melt butter and add apple slices. When apples are coated, add vodka and toss gently for about 3 minutes, until apples become slightly soft. Remove from heat.

To construct, place 1 apple slice on a toast round and spoon about 1 tablespoon of goat cheese on top. When all of them are constructed, place entire cookie sheet under broiler and remove as soon as the top of the goat cheese is slightly browned. Be sure you don't forget them, because they will brown quickly.

STEAK BITES WITH BLOODY MARY DIPPING SAUCE

½ cup Three Olives vodka
1 tbsp. extra-virgin olive oil, plus more for drizzling

1 small onion, finely chopped
2 tbsp. Worcestershire sauce
2 tsp. hot pepper sauce
1 cup tomato sauce
1 rounded tbsp. prepared horseradish
Salt and pepper
1⅓ lbs. beef sirloin cut into large bite-sized pieces (1 by 2 inches)
Steak seasoning blend or coarse salt and black pepper
6- to 8-inch bamboo skewers

Heat a small saucepan over medium heat. Add oil and onions and sauté for 5 minutes. Add vodka and reduce by ½ . Add Worcestershire, hot sauce, tomato sauce and horseradish. Stir to combine the dipping sauce and return the sauce to a bubble. Add salt and pepper and adjust seasonings.

Heat nonstick skillet over high heat. Coat meat bites lightly in oil. Season with steak seasoning blend or salt and pepper, to taste. Cook the meat until caramelized all over, for about 2 minutes on each side. Transfer dipping sauce to a small dish and place at the center of a serving platter. Surround the dip with meat bites and set several bamboo "skewers alongside meat.

"DRUNKEN SHRIMP STYLE" QUICK MARINADE

1 cup Three Olives vodka
Wooden skewers, soaked in water for 20 to 30 minutes
1 cup citrus juice made from freshly squeezed orange, lime, and
    lemon juice
¼ cup peeled ginger, chopped
½ clove garlic, finely minced
Sugar, to taste
1 cup miso paste
½ cup light cooking oil, preferably sesame, canola, or vegetable
1 lb. small shrimp, rinsed, shells intact

½ lb. bay scallops

Soak skewers in water for 45 minutes. In a mixing bowl, combine vodka, citrus, ginger, garlic, sugar, and miso paste and whisk until mixed. Slowly whisk in oil until smooth.

Pour marinade over unpeeled shrimp and scallops. Cover and let marinate in refrigerator for 45 to 60 minutes. Skewer shrimp and scallops (optimally 4 to a skewer) and place on grill over direct heat. Allow tails and legs of shrimp to slightly blacken before turning. Scallops should brown slightly before turning.

BOBBY FLAY'S FRA DIAVOLO JAMBALAYA

½ cup Three Olives vodka
2 red bell peppers
4 plum tomatoes, halved
5 cloves garlic, peeled, plus 3 cloves, thinly sliced
6 tbsp. olive oil
Salt and freshly ground black pepper
1 to 2 tbsp. chipotle puree, depending on how spicy you like it
12 oz. Spanish-style chorizo, sliced in ¼-inch thick slices
1 large Spanish onion, finely chopped
3 cloves garlic, thinly sliced
1 tsp. red pepper flakes
2 cups long-grain white rice
2 to 3 cups lobster stock
1 tbsp. finely chopped fresh oregano leaves
1 lb. cultivated mussels, scrubbed
2 steamed lobsters (1½ lbs. each) meat removed
1 lb. jumbo lump crabmeat
3 tbsp. chopped fresh basil leaves
¼ cup coarsely chopped fresh parsley leaves
¼ cup thinly sliced green onions

Preheat oven to 375° F.

Place the peppers, tomatoes, and 5 garlic cloves on a baking sheet, drizzle with 3 tablespoons of the oil, and season with salt and pepper. Roast until the peppers and tomatoes are slightly charred and the garlic is golden brown. Transfer to a food processor with the chipotle puree and process until smooth, then scrape into a bowl.

Heat a large sauté pan over medium heat. Add the chorizo and cook until golden brown on both sides. Remove with a slotted spoon to a plate lined with paper towels.

Heat the remaining 3 tablespoons of oil in a Dutch oven over high heat. Add the onion and cook until soft. Add the sliced garlic and cook until lightly golden brown. Add the red pepper flakes and cook for 20 seconds. Stir in the rice and cook for 2 minutes.

Add the vodka and cook until reduced. Add the tomato/pepper puree and enough stock to cover, season with salt, and bring to a boil. Add the chorizo and oregano, cover, and cook for 10 minutes. Lift the lid, add the mussels, cover again, and cook until the mussels have opened, discarding any that do not, the rice is al dente and all the liquid is absorbed. Remove from the heat and let sit 5 minutes. Fluff with a fork and stir in the lobster meat and crabmeat, fresh basil, parsley, and green onions.

ROASTED BEET AND SMOKED STURGEON SALAD WITH VODKA VINAIGRETTE

6 tbsp. Three Olives vodka
2 lbs. fresh beets, washed, and tops and stems trimmed
2 tbsp. olive oil
3 tbsp. minced shallots
3 tbsp. red wine vinegar
3 tbsp. extra virgin olive oil
2 tbsp. honey
½ tsp. salt
¼ tsp. freshly ground black pepper

2 tbsp. chopped fresh dill
½ lb. boneless smoked sturgeon, flaked into bite-sized pieces
1 Granny Smith apple, cored and julienned
3 oz. field greens

Preheat oven to 400°F.

In a bowl, toss the beets with the oil. Place on a roasting pan and bake until cooked through but still firm, for about 1 hour. Remove from the oven and cool. When cool enough to handle, peel and cut into ¼-inch thick slices.

In a bowl, whisk together the shallots, red wine vinegar, vodka, olive oil, honey, salt, black pepper, and fresh dill. Add smoked sturgeon, apple, and beets and toss briefly just to combine. Serve on top of field greens.

COLD STRING BEANS WITH VODKA VINAIGRETTE

2 tbsp. Three Olives vodka
1 lb. string beans, trimmed, or 1 lb. asparagus, peeled and trimmed
½ cup olive oil
1 large shallot, finely minced
1 tbsp. Dijon mustard
¼ cup Georgian or balsamic vinegar
1 tbsp. sumac (edible ground sumac is available from Mid-Eastern or Russian markets or a spice shop)
Salt and pepper
2 hardboiled eggs, finely chopped, optional
1 red bell pepper, finely diced, optional

Blanch and refresh string beans in salted water.

In 1 tablespoon olive oil taken from the ½ cup, caramelize the minced shallot.

Put shallot, mustard, vinegar, and vodka in a blender. Slowly drizzle in the remaining oil. Mix in sumac, salt, and pepper. Serve over string beans (or asparagus).

Optional: Garnish with a little chopped hardboiled egg and/or finely diced red bell pepper.

KICKED UP PASTA RAGS WITH VODKA SAUCE

1 cup Three Olives vodka
¼ lb. bacon, cut into ½ -inch pieces
2 cups finely chopped yellow onions
½ tsp. crushed red pepper
2 tbsp. minced garlic
1 (14-oz.) can crushed tomatoes
½ cup fresh or frozen green peas
1 cup heavy cream
⅓ cup chopped basil
4 sheets fresh pasta, (about 1 lb.) torn into rags about 3-inches by
   1-inch each
Grated parmesan, for serving (optional)

Bring a large pot of salted water to a boil.

In a skillet, cook the bacon over medium-high heat until the fat is rendered and just beginning to brown, for about 4 minutes. Add the onions and crushed red pepper and sauté until soft and slightly caramelized, for about 6 minutes. Add the garlic and cook for 1 minute. Add the tomatoes and stir well to combine. Cook for 2 minutes, stirring. Add the vodka and cook until slightly reduced, for about 3 to 4 minutes. Add the peas and cream, and cook until thickened, about 2 minutes. Remove from heat and stir in the basil.

Cook the pasta in the boiling water until just al dente, about 2 minutes. Drain in a colander. Add to the pasta sauce, and toss to combine. Serve immediately with grated parmesan, if desired.

VODKA CURED RED SNAPPER

⅓ cup Three Olives vodka
3 tbsp. fresh orange juice
3 tbsp. fresh lime juice
¼ cup finely chopped red bell pepper
3 tbsp. finely chopped red onions
2 tbsp. chopped cilantro
1 tsp. minced garlic
½ tsp. minced habanero
1 lb. red snapper fillets, cut into ½-inch cubes
2 tsp. kosher salt

In a bowl, combine the vodka, orange juice, lime juice, bell pepper, onions, cilantro, garlic, and pepper.

Ten to fifteen minutes before serving, fold the fish and salt into the vodka cure. Divide the fish and any juices among 4 to 6 decorative bowls or glasses, and serve immediately.

WHITE AND GREEN ASPARAGUS WITH SEVRUGA CAVIAR AND VODKA CRÈME FRAICHE

1 tbsp. vodka
8 white asparagus
8 green asparagus
1 oz. Sevruga caviar
4 oz. smoked salmon
½ tbsp. lemon rind julienne
4 tbsp. crème fraiche
3 dashes of lemon juice

Put asparagus in two separate saucepans in a small amount of boiling water. Cover and cook and/or steam until they begin to smell, for about

3 minutes. They should still be crisp. Once cooked, refresh them under boiling water.

Cut the asparagus in half lengthwise and remove the soft pulp along the center, trying to create a dent. Carefully fill the cavity along the length of the asparagus with caviar and keep cold. Make 4 salmon roses and set them aside on a plate. To make salmon roses: Slice salmon very thin. Start with first piece and roll tightly to form cone, add another piece of salmon to outside of cone and continue until salmon piece forms a rose.

Combine the crème fraiche with the vodka, lemon juice, and lemon peel. Mix well.

Place 2 white asparagus and 2 green asparagus on each plate. Garnish with a salmon rose and some crème fraiche.

ABSOLUT VODKA CURED SALMON WITH BLOOD ORANGE JUICE AND LIME

2 tbsp. Absolut vodka
16 thin slices raw salmon
2 shallots, finely chopped
1 leek, finely chopped into 3 mm/ 1/8 in pieces
Juice of 1 ripe blood orange
1 tsp. sea salt
Freshly milled black pepper
Few sprigs mizuono leaves or rocket
Juice of 1 lime to finish

Lay out the thin slices of salmon on plates, 4 per plate. Sprinkle each plate evenly with shallot and leek.

Mix together the vodka and orange juice, divide into 4 equal portions, and trickle 1 portion onto each plate to cover the salmon. Just before serving, sprinkle lightly with sea salt and freshly ground black pepper and lime juice. Garnish with mizuono leaves and serve immediately.

VODKA-SPIKED GAZPACHO

¼ cup vodka (Finlandia, Seagram's Imported, Smirnoff, Stolichnaya, Absolut)
2 tbsp. ripe tomatoes, cored and chopped
1 small red onion, chopped
2 scallions, chopped
1 hot or mild green chili, chopped
2 garlic cloves, finely minced
1 small cucumber, chopped
¼ cup chopped coriander leaves
2 tbsp. chopped fresh basil leaves
Juice of 1 lime
¼ cup olive oil
salt and freshly ground pepper, to taste
1 ripe avocado, sliced
Sour cream, optional
Croutons, optional

In a large serving bowl, combine all ingredients except avocado, sour cream, and croutons. Adjust seasonings to taste. Serve with an avocado slice, a dollop of sour cream, and a few croutons, if desired. Serves 6.

SEARED SCALLOPS AND PEARS WITH LEMON-VODKA SAUCE

For the seared scallops and pears:
2 tbsp. olive oil
2 tsp. unsalted butter
8 oz. large sea scallops
2 large ripe Bartlett, Anjou, or Bosc pears, cored, peeled, and halved
8 oz. fresh fettuccine or 4 oz. dried fettuccine

For the lemon vodka sauce:
2 tbsp. vodka
1 lemon, grated zest and juice of ½ cup heavy cream
1 tbsp. chopped fresh chives
Salt and freshly ground black pepper, to taste
3 pieces of fresh chives, for garnish
Julienned lemon zest, for garnish

To make the seared scallops and pears:

Heat 1 tablespoon of oil and 1 teaspoon of butter in a 10-inch skillet over medium heat until the butter foams, then sauté the scallops for about 2–3 minutes per side, or until golden, turning once. Transfer to a warmed plate, cover, set aside, and keep warm. Wipe out the pan with a paper towel, then add the remaining 1 tablespoon oil and 1 teaspoon butter, and heat over medium-high heat until the butter foams.

Place the pears in the pan cut-side-down, and sauté until golden, for about 2–3 minutes. Turn and cook the rounded side until golden. Remove from heat and keep warm.

At the same time, fill a 4-quart pot with salted water and bring it to a full boil. Drop the fettuccine into the boiling water and cook for about 2 minutes if using fresh fettuccine, or for about 8 minutes if using dried fettuccine, or until al dente. Drain.

To make the lemon vodka sauce:

Mix the lemon zest and juice and set aside. Combine the cream and vodka in small saucepan and boil for 3 minutes. Add the chives and mixed juice and zest. Boil for 1 minute or until thickened.

To assemble:

Toss the hot pasta with the sauce. Divide between two warmed dinner plates. Top with seared scallops and season with salt and pepper. Arrange two pear halves on either side of the scallops on each plate. Garnish with chive pieces and lemon zest and serve at once. Serves 2.

ABSOLUT-LY HOT BBQ RIBS

½ cup Absolut Peppar vodka
3 lbs. pork spareribs
Salt and freshly ground black pepper, to taste
½ cup chopped onions
1 tsp. minced garlic
1 tbsp. unsalted butter
1 cup tomato puree
⅓ cup granulated sugar
2 tbsp. cider vinegar
2 tbsp. Worcestershire sauce
1 tbsp. prepared brown mustard
¼ tsp. red pepper flakes

Preheat oven to 400° F and season spareribs with salt and pepper to taste. Place ribs on a rack in a roasting pan.

In a heavy saucepan, sauté onions and garlic in the butter for about 5 minutes over medium heat, or until onions are translucent. Add remaining ingredients and simmer over low heat for 5 minutes, until slightly thickened.

Bake ribs for 30 minutes. Reduce heat to 350° F and bake for 1 hour. Brush ribs with sauce. Bake for another 15 minutes. Turn ribs, brush with more sauce, and bake for an additional 15 minutes. Serve with remaining sauce on the side. Serves about 6.

Tip: Try this barbeque sauce on other meats, such as chicken and pork chops.

FETTUCCINI ABSOLUT PEPPAR VODKA

¼ cup Absolut Peppar vodka
1 lb. fettuccini
1½ cups peas, fresh cooked or frozen
¼ lb. chopped prosciutto

2 ¼ tsp. rubbed sage cloves garlic, chopped
2 tbsp. butter
2 cups cream
Pecorino or parmesan cheese, to taste
Salt and pepper, to taste

In a large skillet add 1 tablespoon of butter, melt. Add prosciutto and peas, then garlic. Sauté until there is a strong garlic aroma. Remove from heat and add Absolut Peppar vodka. Reduce liquid by half, then add cream. Simmer slowly. Add cooked fettuccini to this mixture. Finish seasoning with sage, salt, pepper, butter and lastly cheese. Serves 6–8.

FLANK STEAK WITH CHIMICHURRI SAUCE

¼ cup Absolut Peppar vodka
1 flank steak, about 2 lbs., (½ inch thick)
½ cup vegetable oil
½ cup malt vinegar
¼ cup water
3 tbsp. chopped fresh parsley
1 tbsp. chopped fresh cilantro (Chinese parsley)
3 cloves garlic, minced
2 jalapeño peppers, roasted, seeded, and minced
½ tsp. salt
¼ tsp. freshly ground pepper

Note: This recipe should be started one day in advance.

Using a sharp knife, score flank steak on each side, about ⅛ inch deep, in a diamond pattern. Place in shallow glass or ceramic dish.

Prepare chimichurri sauce by combining remaining ingredients in a medium bowl. Coat each side of flank steak with ¼ cup sauce. Cover and refrigerate overnight. Place the remaining sauce in glass jar with a tight-fitting lid. Let stand at room temperature for 24 hours.

Remove flank steak from refrigerator one hour before cooking. Grill over very hot coals or cook under very hot broiler for about three minutes per side. (Flank steak must be served medium-rare to rare.) Carve immediately by cutting across grain into slices about ¼ inch thick. Serve with remaining chimichurri sauce.

Note: Flank steak will toughen as it cools. It should be carved as soon as it is cooked, even if served at room temperature.

ABSOLUT-LY DELICIOUS CAKE

¼ cup Absolut vodka
1 tbsp. plus 1 tsp. unflavored gelatin
½ cup boiling water
¼ cup sugar
1 can frozen orange juice concentrate
1 cup sour cream
2 egg whites, stiffly beaten
1 (8-inch) layer of any plain cake
1 cup canned mandarin orange sections, for garnish
½ cup green maraschino cherries, for garnish

Soften gelatin in Absolut vodka, then dissolve in boiling water. Add sugar and orange juice and chill until mixture begins to set. Add sour cream and egg whites and beat with rotary beater until fluffy. Line an oiled 8-inch spring from pan with 1-inch slices of cake. Pour gelatin mixture over cake and chill in refrigerator until firm. At serving time, garnish with mandarin orange sections and cherries cut into leaf shapes.

SWEDISH MOCHA ICE CREAM SAUCE

¼ cup Absolut vodka
2 oz. semi-sweet chocolate, chopped very fine
¼ cup water
¼ cup corn syrup

½ cup heavy (whipping) cream
½ cup granulated sugar
1 tbsp. instant coffee powder (regular strength)

Bring water, corn syrup, Absolut vodka, heavy cream, and sugar to a boil in a small saucepan over low heat. Remove from heat. Add instant coffee and whisk until well dissolved. Add chopped chocolate; stir until melted and smooth. Let sauce cool to room temperature to thicken. Sauce can be used warm or thinner consistency. Yields 1 cup.

THREE BEAN SALAD AND THEN SOME

½ cup Absolut vodka
1 lb. can waxed beans
1 lb. can green beans
1 lb. can red kidney beans
½ cup French dressing made with tarragon vinegar
Freshly ground pepper to taste

Drain the cans of beans; mix well with the French dressing. Refrigerate 1 hour. Pour in the vodka, mix well, and refrigerate for several hours. Before serving, dust with freshly ground pepper. Serves 8–10 as an appetizer.

PEPPARED FRIED RICE

1 piece green onion, chopped
1 egg
2 cups cooked rice

"A"
1 oz. Absolut Peppar vodka
1 oz. B.B.Q. pork, diced
1 oz. baby shrimp
1 oz. cooked chicken, diced

1 oz. green peas
1 oz. white onion, chopped

"B"
½ tsp. chicken powder
1 tsp. soy sauce
Salt and pepper to taste

Heat the wok until hot, then add 2½ tablespoons oil, add the egg to stir fry; cook until the egg is well done. Place it together with rice.

Reheat the wok, add 1½ tablespoons oil, then add "A" to stir fry for a few seconds, add the cooked rice and egg, and add "B" to taste. When the rice is hot, add the green onion.

ABSOLUT CITRON GUACAMOLE

2 tbsp. Absolut Citron vodka
4 ripe avocados
1 cup plain yogurt
½ cup red onion, chopped
½ cup salsa
½ clove garlic
1 tbsp. lemon juice
Salt to taste

Peel avocados. Add remaining ingredients. Stir with fork just enough to break up avocados. Chill and serve.

GLAZED HAM WITH SMIRNOFF PINEAPPLE SAUCE

½ cup Smirnoff vodka
4-5 lb. precooked boneless ham
Whole cloves

1 cup brown sugar
½ cup maple syrup
2 tbsp. Dijon mustard
1 tbsp. cornstarch
1 can crushed pineapple (1 lb. 4 oz.)

Stud surface of ham with cloves. Place on rack in shallow baking pan. Bake in 350° F oven. Follow directions on ham packaging for length of baking time.

Meanwhile, combine sugar, maple syrup, mustard, and ¼ cup vodka. Use ¾ cup glaze to baste ham every 10 minutes during last 30–45 minutes of baking. Stir cornstarch into remaining glaze in saucepan. Add pineapple with juice. Simmer, stirring constantly until sauce thickens. Stir in remaining Smirnoff vodka. Serve sauce with ham.

ABSOLUT CITRON OVEN BAKED COD

4 tbsp. Absolut Citron vodka
1 large white onion, thinly sliced
1 tbsp. oil
1 cup cooked carrots, sliced
1½ lbs. cod, cut into 8 serving pieces
½ tsp. salt, more to taste
Pinch dry marjoram
Pinch black pepper
Pinch allspice
1 cup light cream
½ cup dry breadcrumbs
2 tbsp. fresh chopped parsley
8 lemon wedges, thinly sliced

Sauté the onion in the oil over medium heat until soft but not browned. Layer the cooked onions and carrots in a small casserole. Sprinkle the cod with vodka, salt, marjoram, allspice, and pepper. Place the cod on top of the vegetables in the casserole. Cover with the cream. Sprinkle with the breadcrumbs.

Bake for 10 to 15 minutes at 375° F until the cod is flaky and lightly browned. Sprinkle with freshly chopped parsley. Serve with lemon wedges and boiled new potatoes. Serves 4 main courses or 8 first course servings.

SPICY THAI-STYLE CHICKEN SALAD

For spicy lemon dressing:
2 tbsp. Absolut Citron vodka
½ cup water
1 tbsp. low-sodium soy sauce
1 tbsp. sugar
1 fresh hot chile pepper, such as jalapeño, seeded (or more to taste)
2 cloves garlic, peeled

For chicken salad:
5 chicken breast halves (about 3¼ lbs.), bone-in, skin-on
½ tsp. salt, plus more to taste
2 medium carrots, shredded
2 scallions, chopped
⅓ cup chopped fresh cilantro, mint or parsley (or a combination)
Freshly ground pepper, to taste
Fresh lettuce leaves

To make spicy lemon dressing:
In a blender, combine all ingredients. Pour into a bowl, cover and refrigerate.

To make the chicken salad:
Place the chicken breasts in a large saucepan. Add water to cover, then stir in the salt. Bring to a boil over high heat. Reduce the heat to medium-low, cover, and simmer for 20 minutes. Remove from heat and let stand, covered, for 1 hour. Drain (reserve the cooking liquid for

another use, if desired) and discard the skin and bones. Using your fingers, shred the chicken breast meat and cool completely. Yields about four cups.

To assemble:
In a large bowl, combine the chicken, carrots, scallions, and cilantro. Add the spicy lemon dressing and toss well. Cover and refrigerate for at least 1 hour. Season with salt and pepper to taste.

Arrange the lettuce leaves on a serving platter. Heap the chicken salad on the lettuce and serve immediately. Serves 4.

STEAMED SHRIMP WITH FINLANDIA LIME VODKA

1 cup Finlandia lime vodka
½ cup water
1 tsp. salt
1 tsp. pepper
1 lb. pink shrimp

Place ingredients into saucepan. Bring to boil. Place 1 pound of pink shrimp (unfrozen) into steamer. Place steamer on top of boiling saucepan. Steam for 10 minutes.

VODKA COCKTAIL SAUCE

1 oz. vodka
8 oz. ketchup
1 oz. prepared horseradish
1 lemon, juice & zest
1 tbs. Worcestershire sauce
Fresh ground pepper

SCREWDRIVER CAKE WITH FINLANDIA VODKA

For cake:
½ cup Finlandia vodka
1 18.25 oz. package yellow cake mix
1 3.5 oz. package instant vanilla pudding mix
¾ cup orange juice
¼ cup vegetable oil
3 eggs

For orange glaze:
½ cup confectioners sugar
3 tbs. orange juice

To make cake:
Preheat oven to 350°F. Grease and flour a 10-inch bundt pan. In a large bowl combine ingredients. Beat until smooth. Pour into prepared bundt pan. Bake at 350° for 45 minutes or until toothpick inserted into middle comes out clean. Cool for 10 minutes in pan, then turn out onto wire rack. Glaze with orange glaze.

To make orange glaze:
In a medium bowl, combine 3 tbsp. orange juice and confectioners sugar. Mix well and pour over cake.

PENNE IN FINLANDIA VODKA SAUCE

¾ cup Finlandia vodka
2 dried red peppers
2⅔ cups whipping cream
10 tbs. butter
6 oz. fresh ripe tomato, seeded and chopped
1 lb. penne
¾ cup parmesan, grated

3 tbs. fresh parsley, minced
Pepper to taste

Soak red peppers in vodka for 24 hours. Combine cream, butter and tomatoes in large heavy saucepan. Simmer until reduced by ⅓, about 12 minutes. Cook pasta according to directions. Drain and add red sauce. Boil 1 minute, stirring constantly. Discard red peppers and add vodka to pasta. Simmer until sauce thickens, stirring constantly, about 3 minutes. Mix in parmesan and parsley, and serve immediately.

TOMATO BRUSCHETTA WITH FINLANDIA VODKA

2 tsp. Finlandia vodka
6 roma tomatoes, finely diced
2 garlic cloves, crushed and minced
2 green onions, finely chopped
½ cup basil leaves, finely shredded
4 tsp. olive oil
Salt & freshly ground pepper

Combine all ingredients and let stand for 30 minutes before serving on sliced and toasted baguette.

FINNISH CHICKEN WITH FINLANDIA VODKA

1 cup Finlandia vodka
1 chicken (about 3½ pounds)
1 tsp. salt
2 ripe tomatoes
1 cup sour cream
1 tsp. pepper, freshly ground
1 clove garlic

1 tsp. fresh chives, snipped
¼ cup butter
¼ cup fresh parsley, snipped
1 tsp. poultry seasoning

Wash and dry chicken, inside and out. Cut into serving pieces. Peel, seed, and chop tomatoes. Peel and mince garlic. In a large skillet, melt the butter and brown the chicken pieces. Set them aside. To the skillet add the tomatoes, garlic, chives, poultry seasoning, salt, pepper, and vodka; blend over low heat. Place the chicken in a large casserole with all skillet ingredients. Bake, covered, in a 325° F oven for 1 hour. Remove the casserole from oven and gently stir in the sour cream. Return to oven. Bake 15 to 20 minutes longer, uncovered. Serves 4.

OYSTER STEW WITH VODKA

2 oz. vodka
12 oysters, shucked
1 shallot, chopped
1 cup heavy cream
1 tbs. chives
1 diced potato (boiled)

Sauté shallot in butter; add vodka and oysters and flambé for seconds. Add cream and potato. Reduce until thick. Spoon over baguette and garnish with chives.

PENNE ALA STILTON SAUCE

4 oz. vodka
1 lb. penne
8 oz. tomato sauce
8 oz. cream

1 oz. garlic, fresh
1 oz. onion, small dice
Basil
Parmesan cheese
8 oz. Stilton cheese

Sauté garlic and onion in olive oil. Add vodka, tomato sauce, and cream. Cook until incorporated and reduce. Finish with fresh basil, parmesan, and crumbled Stilton. Toss over penne.

VODKA CEVICHE COCKTAIL

2 oz. vodka
1 filet of fresh snapper, scallops, and shrimp
1 habanero pepper, diced
¼ cup fresh cilantro, diced
1 red pepper, small dice
1 red onion, small dice
Juice of 1 lemon and 1 lime

Dice fish, scallops, and shrimp. Combine all ingredients. Chill and serve.

FETTUCCINI WITH DUNGENESS CRAB WITH SKYY VODKA ESSENCE

8 oz. Skyy vodka
1 lb. fettuccini pasta
8 oz. cooked Dungeness crab meat
¼ cup shallots, sliced
2 sprigs thyme, fresh
1 bay leaf
6 oz. butter
1 tsp. olive oil

2 tbs. chives, chopped
Salt and pepper

In a stainless-steel pot, place olive oil, shallots, bay leaf, and thyme and sweat over low heat for about 7 minutes. Make sure there is no brown color in the pot. Add the vodka and reduce heat by two thirds.

Whisk in the butter slowly until emulsified. Strain the sauce through a fine strainer, then add the chopped chives to the sauce.

Cook the pasta in salted boiling water until al dente. Drain the pasta, place in a mixing bowl and add the sauce and the cooked, picked crab meat. Serves 4.

⚜ Recipe by Rabah Abubaltan, Chef de Cuisine, One Market Restaurant, San Francisco, and courtesy of Skyy Spirits.

INFERNO QUACAMOLE

2 tbs. Inferno Pepper Pot vodka
2 ripe avocados
1 tbs. finely chopped onion
1 tomato, peeled, seeded, and chopped
1 tsp. finely chopped coriander
½ tsp. salt

Peel, chop, and mash avocados to a puree, then add all other ingredients and mix well. Cover with aluminum foil to prevent discoloration, and refrigerate. Serve with raw vegetables or toasted tortillas. Makes about 2 cups.

⚜ Recipe courtesy of Kittling Ridge Estate Wines & Spirits, makers of Inferno Pepper Pot vodka.

WARM OYSTERS WITH SKYY VODKA LEMON ESSENCE

½ cup Skyy vodka
24 Long Island oysters
1 tbs. Meyer lemon juice
½ tbs. cracked black pepper
2 tbs. sliced shallots
½ tbs. minced garlic
1 tbs. chopped cilantro
4 sprigs cilantro
¼ lb. butter
1 tbs. olive oil

Place the olive oil in a stainless steel pot and sweat down shallots and garlic without any caramelization. Add the vodka and lemon juice, and reduce by two thirds. Add butter and whisk to emulsify.

Next add cracked pepper and the chopped cilantro to the sauce. Place the shucked oysters in a 450° F oven for 4 minutes or until warmed through. Place the sauce on top of the oysters, garnish with cilantro sprigs, and serve. Serves 4.

⁂ Recipe by Rabah Abusbaltan, Chef de Cuisine, One Market Restaurant, San Francisco, CA, and courtesy of Skyy Spirits.

DEVILISH MUSSELS

2–3 oz. Inferno Pepper Pot vodka
2 lbs. mussels, cleaned
1 green bell pepper, chopped
1 large white onion, chopped
3 cloves garlic, minced
3–4 tomatoes peeled, seeded, and chopped
3 cups chicken stock
1 cup celery, chopped

1 cup chopped parsley
½ cup green onions, chopped
¼ cup fresh basil, chopped
Salt and pepper, to taste
Tabasco

In a large pot, sauté garlic and onions over medium heat, until onions are transparent. Add celery, bell pepper, and tomatoes and cook 10 minutes over medium heat. Add chicken stock and vodka, stirring well. Add parsley, basil, green onions, salt, pepper, and Tabasco.

Bring to a slow boil, and add mussels to the pot. Cook over medium heat until the shells of the mussels open completely, indicating that they are done. Remove from heat and allow mussels to stand for 10 minutes to absorb all the flavors. Serve over rice or pasta. Serves 2 to 3.

⚜ Recipe courtesy of Kittling Ridge Estate Wines & Spirits makers of Inferno Pepper Pot vodka.

VODKA-MARINATED SALMON

1 oz. vodka
1 lb. salmon
⅓ oz. chopped juniper berries
½ tsp. saffron
¾ oz. chopped dill
⅔ cup granulated sugar
⅓ cup sea salt

Fillet the salmon, leaving the skin on. Sprinkle vodka, juniper berries, saffron, and dill over the flesh of the salmon. Make a mix of the salt and sugar; sprinkle some over the salmon. Place the fish in a non-reactive container, flesh side up, and sprinkle with the remainder of the salt and sugar mix. Fill the container with water to cover the salmon, cover with plastic, and allow to marinate in a warm place overnight. Serve with black caviar and crème fraiche. Serves 4.

✤ Recipe courtesy of Klaus Kochendoerfer, Executive Chef, Grand Hotel Europe, St. Petersburg.

STOLI'S LOBSTER-SHRIMP FETTUCINE

2 oz. Stolichnaya vodka
3 jumbo shrimp
2 oz. lobster tail meat, cut in cubes
1 oz. shallots, finely chopped
1 clove fresh garlic, finely chopped
1 oz. zucchini, julienne cut
4 strings saffron
1 oz. tomato concassee
½ oz. fresh spinach, julienne cut
1 oz. brie cheese, shredded
4 oz. heavy cream
2 tsp. olive oil
4 oz. fettuccine, cooked *al dente*
Salt and pepper
Lemon juice
Worcestershire sauce

Marinate shrimp and lobster with lemon juice and a few drops of Worcestershire sauce. Heat 1 tsp. olive oil in a pan and sauté lobster and shrimp at medium heat. Season with salt and pepper while cooking. Remove seafood from pan and set aside.

In same pan, add shallots, ½ clove of garlic and zucchini and sauté for two minutes. Remove from pan and set aside. Fill same pan with vodka and bring to a boil. Add heavy cream. Add saffron and bring to a boil. Add seafood and heat up and then set aside.

Heat olive oil in a second pan. Add the rest of the garlic and spinach. Sauté for ½ minute. Season with salt and pepper.

Cook fettuccine in boiling water. Strain and add to seafood. Put pan with seafood back on the stove. Heat up and mix pasta with sauce. Arrange a circle in the center of the plate with the spinach and fill with pasta. Cut shrimp in halves and arrange on plate. Garnish with tomato concassee. Serves 2.

⊕ Recipe by Frank Weber, Executive Chef, Norwegian Cruise Line S/S Norway

LEMON SORBET

2 oz. Finlandia vodka
2 cups lemon juice
2 cups Caster sugar
Lemon peel
2 egg whites, whisked stiff

Bring the sugar, lemon, and lemon peel to a boil. Cool. Add vodka and pour into an ice-cream machine. When the mixture is nearly frozen, add the egg whites and continue freezing until ready. Pour a little vodka into the serving dish and decorate with lemon balm.

P.S. GAZPACHO

¼ cup Absolut Peppar vodka
2 medium cucumbers, peeled, seeded, and cut into small chunks
3 large ripe tomatoes, peeled, seeded and quartered
1 carrot, peeled, and cut into small slices
1 green pepper, cut into small chunks
1 red pepper, cut into small chunks
½ medium onion, cut into quarters
1 clove garlic
⅓ cup packed fresh parsley leaves
⅓ cup packed fresh basil leaves (or 2 tsp. dried)
2 cups V-8 juice
3 dashes Worcestershire sauce
2 dashes Angostura bitters

Low-fat yogurt for garnish
Salt and pepper to taste

Puree all ingredients together in batches in the blender until mixture reaches a smooth consistency. Pour into a bowl and stir in vodka. Cover and refrigerate overnight. Serve in large hollowed tomato with a spoonful of low-fat yogurt. Serves 8.

CELERY HEARTS AND HEARTS OF PALM

¾ cup Gordon's vodka
4 bunches celery
1½ cups chicken broth
½ cup mayonnaise, preferably homemade
4 pieces canned heart of palm
3 cups shredded lettuce
¾ cup thinly sliced almonds
¼ cup diced pimento

Wash the bunches of celery. Remove the outer stalks and tops; reserve for another purpose. Cut each heart in half lengthwise. In a large skillet heat the chicken broth and ½ cup of the vodka. Cook the celery hearts in this mixture until they are tender. When done, turn off heat and remove the celery from the skillet, being careful to keep the hearts intact. Set aside to cool. When cool, refrigerate.

Reheat the liquid in the skillet and reduce by one half. Pour the liquid into a small mixing bowl; refrigerate. When cool, stir in the mayonnaise. When well blended, stir in the remaining ¼ cup of vodka. Blend well and refrigerate until serving time.

To serve, place one celery heart and one heart of palm on shredded lettuce. Sprinkle with sliced almonds and diced pimento; sauce with the mayonnaise. Serves 4 as an appetizer.

SWEDISH MOCHA ICE CREAM SAUCE

2 oz. Absolut vodka
2 oz. semi-sweet chocolate, chopped very finely
¼ cup water
¼ cup corn syrup
¼ cup heavy (whipping) cream
½ cup granulated sugar
1 tbs. instant coffee powder (regular strength)

Bring water, corn syrup, vodka, heavy cream, and sugar to a boil in a small saucepan over low heat. Remove from heat. Add instant coffee and whisk until well dissolved. Add chopped chocolate and stir until melted and smooth. Let sauce cool to room temperature to thicken. Sauce can be used warm at thinner consistency. Yields one cup.

ABSOLUTELY DELICIOUS CAKE

¼ cup Absolut vodka
1 tbs. plus 1 tsp. unflavored gelatin
½ cup boiling water
¼ cup sugar
1 can frozen concentrated orange juice
1 cup sour cream
2 egg whites, stiffly beaten
1 8-inch layer of any plain cake
1 cup canned Mandarin orange sections for garnish
½ cup green Maraschino cherries for garnish

Soften gelatin in vodka, then dissolve in boiling water. Add sugar and orange juice and chill until mixture begins to set. Add sour cream and egg whites and beat with rotary beater until fluffy. Line an oiled 8-inch spring form pan with 1-inch slices of cake. Pour gelatin mixture over cake and chill in refrigerator until firm. At serving time, garnish with mandarin orange sections and cherries cut into leaf shapes.

50

VODKA PRODUCTION FACTS

Downunder vodka is an 80-proof vodka distilled and bottled in Melbourne, Australia.

Iceberg vodka is produced in Reykjavik, Iceland.

Pearl vodka is produced in Alberta, Canada.

Danzka vodka is produced in Denmark.

Turi vodka is the only super-premium vodka created, sourced, and distilled in Estonia.

Finlandia vodka is produced in Helsinki, Finland.

Cîroc vodka is manufactured in France.

Roberto Cavalli vodka is produced entirely in Italy.

Grey Goose is produced in France.

Jean-Marc XO vodka is a premium vodka produced in France.

Ursus Roter vodka is a red vodka made in Iceland.

Ketel One vodka is made at the Nolet Distillery in Schiedam, Netherlands.

Van Gogh vodka is handcrafted at the Royal Dirkzwager Distillery in Schiedam, Holland.

Vox vodka is a product of the Netherlands.

Christiania vodka is manufactured in Norway.

Bols vodka is produced in Poland.

Chopin vodka is produced in the Polish region of Podlasie.

Wyborowa vodka is a popular brand produced in Poland.

Żubrówka vodka is manufactured in the region of the contemporary Polish-Belarusian.

The Jewel of Russia vodka is produced in Russia.

Russian Standard vodka is produced in a distillery in St. Petersburg, Russia.

SV the Silk vodka is produced in their distillery located in Ruza, outside of Moscow.

Absolut vodka is a Swedish brand owned by V&S Group, and produced at their facilities near Åhus, Scania in southern Sweden.

Fris vodka is produced in Denmark.

Level vodka is produced in Ahus, Sweden.

Three Olives vodka is an ultra-premium vodka that is produced in England.

3 Vodka is an American brand manufactured by New York-based Sovereign Brands, LLC.

Hangar One vodka is an artisan vodka produced in Alameda, California.

Popov vodka is produced by British drinks giant Diageo plc's Diageo North American subsidiary. It is manufactured in Stamford, Connecticut.

Shakers vodka is produced in Benson, Minnesota by Infinite Spirits.

Skyy vodka is produced by Skyy Spirits LLC in San Francisco, California.

Belvedere vodka is from Poland.

Tito's Handmade vodka is produced in Austin, Texas, and created by Bert Butler "Tito" Beveridge.

Triple Eight vodka is produced in Nantucket Island, Massachusetts.

Han vodka is produced in South Korea.

Boru vodka is produced in Ireland.

Smirnoff vodka is produced in the United States.

Svedka vodka is manufactured in Lidköping, Sweden.

Perfect 1864 vodka is produced in France, at Grandes Distilleries Peureux de Fougerolles.

Oso Negro vodka, Spanish for "black bear," is brewed and bottled in Mexico.

Zodiac vodka is distilled and bottled in Idaho.

Monopolowa vodka is made in Austria.

Rachmaninoff vodka is a German-produced vodka.

Reyka vodka is notable for being the first vodka distilled in Iceland.

Exclusiv vodka is produced in Moldova.

Stolichnaya vodka is produced in Tambov, Russia.

Xellent vodka is produced in Switzerland.

Trump vodka is distilled at the Wanders Distillery in Holland.

Gotham vodka is produced in the United States.

Blavod vodka is produced in the United Kingdom.

100
VODKA WEBSITES

http://www.267.com/
http://www.360vodka.com
http://www.42below.co.nz
http://www.888vodka.com/

http://www.absolutvodka.com
http://www.adamba.com/Spirytus

http://www.bartonbrands.com/mrbostonvodka.html
http://www.beyondvodka.com
http://www.bisonbrandvodka.net/
http://www.blackvodka.com
http://www.blueicevodka.com
http://www.boru.com
http://www.burnettsvodka.com

http://www.cardinalvodka.com/
http://www.castlebrandsinc.com
http://www.caviarwodka.com
http://www.charbay.com/
http://www.chopinvodka.com
http://www.christianiavodka.com

http://www.cocktailtimes.com/vodka/
http://coldrivervodka.com/
http://www.cristall.com

http://www.danzka.com/
http://www.drinksamericas.com/brands/trump.htm

http://www.effenvodka.com/
http://www.extremebeverage.com/pe/productHome.php

http://www.finlandia-vodka.com
http://frisvodka.com

http://www.glaciervodka.com
http://www.goldenbarr.com
http://www.greygoosevodka.com

http://www.hamptonsvodka.com
http://www.hanasianvodka.com/
http://www.hangarone.com
http://www.happyvodka.com
http://www.heaven-hill.com/brands-vodka.html
http://www.herbsvodka.com/
http://www.hrdspirits.com/

http://www.iceberg.net
http://idolvodka.com/
http://www.ivodka.com/zubrowka-poland.html

http://www.jaguarvodka.com/
http://www.jewelofrussia.com
http://www.jmxo.com/
http://www.johnnylovevodka.com/

http://www.kamericas.com/Charodei.htm
http://www.ketelone.com

http://www.lairdandcompany.com/
http://leveldrinks.com/
http://www.lipsimport.com/
http://www.luksusova.com

http://www.makovodka.com
http://www.mccormickdistilling.com/mccormick_family.html
http://www.mcmahonvodka.com/
http://www.medoff.co.uk/
http://www.minivodkaguy.com/vodka17.html

http://www.orangev.com/

http://patriotvodka.com/
http://www.pearlvodka.com
http://www.polmos.torun.pl
http://pravdavodka.com

http://www.rainvodka.com
http://www.redarmy.com
http://www.rocketfuel.co.uk
http://www.rockymountainvodka.com/44north.html
http://rothvodka.com/

http://www.russianstandard.com/
http://www.russianvodkahouse.com

http://www.skyy.com
http://www.smirnoff.com
http://squareonevodka.com/
http://www.stoli.com
http://www.stonvodka.com/
http://www.svedka.com
http://www.svvodka.com
http://www.tanqueray.com/

http://www.theinvodka.com/
http://www.threeolives.com/
http://www.titosvodka.com
http://www.tommygunsvodka.com/

http://www.uk5.0rg/
http://www.ultimatvodka.com
http://www.uvvodka.com/

http://v2vodka.com/
http://www.vangoghvodka.com
http://www.vermontspirits.com/pr_white.html
http://www.vinpol.com.pl/ang/

http://vodka.com/
http://www.vodka360.com
http://www.vodkabrands.com/
http://www.vodkasobieski.com
http://www.voxvodka.com

http://www.wodka-gorbatschow.de/flash.php
http://www.wyborowa.com

http://www.xellent.ch/
http://xratedvodka.com/

http://www.yesimportedvodka.com/

http://www.znaps.com
http://www.zodiacspirits.com
http://zyrvodka.com/

GLOSSARY

TOOLS YOU WILL NEED

Bar spoon: A long spoon for stirring cocktails or pitchers.

Blender: Blending drinks or crushing ice. Remember to save your blade by always pouring in the liquid before the ice.

Cocktail shaker and mixing/measuring glass: There are countless designs to choose from, but the standard is the Boston. It's a mixing glass that fits snugly into a stainless steel cone.

Ice bag: To crush ice use a rubber mallet and a lint free or canvas ice bag, often referred to as a Lewis Ice Bag.

Ice bucket: Should have a vacuum seal and the ability to hold three trays of ice.

Ice scoop/tongs/ice pick: Never use your hands to pick up ice; use a scoop or tongs. The ice pick can help you unstick ice or break it up.

Jigger/measuring glass: Glass or metal, all drinks should be made using these bar tools. Remember that drinks on the rocks and mixed drinks should contain no more than 2 oz. of alcohol.

Knife and cutting board: A sturdy board and a small, very sharp paring knife are essential to cutting fruit garnishes.

Muddler: Use this small wooden bat or pestle to crush fruit, herbs, or cracked ice. Muddlers come in all different sizes and are used for making Stixx drinks.

Napkins/coasters: To place a drink on, hold a drink with, and for basic convenience.

Pitcher of water: Keep it clean. Someone always wants water and you certainly will use it.

Pourer: A helpful way to pour directly into the glass. A lidded spout helps keep everything but the drink out.

Stirrers/straws: Use them to sip, stir, and mix drinks. Glass is preferred for the mixer/stirrer.

Strainer: The strainer, quite simply, prevents ice from pouring out of the shaker. The two most common types in use are the Hawthorne, with its distinctive coil rim it is most often used when pouring from the metal part of the Boston Shaker, and the Julep, a perforated metal spoon like strainer used when pouring from the glass part of the Boston.

Swizzle stick: A fancy stirrer, often times with the establishment's name on it.

Wine/bottle opener: They come in all shapes and sizes, the best is the industry standard waiter's opener. It can open cans as well as snap off those bottle tops and has a sharp blade.

GLASSWARE

Brandy snifters: Smaller sizes of the glasses, which come in sizes ranging from 5½ to 22 oz., are perfect for serving cognac, liqueurs and premium whiskeys. The larger sizes provide enough space for a noseful of aroma and the small stems on large bowls allow a cupped hand to warm the liquid.

Champagne glass: A narrow version of the standard wine glass has a tapered bowl to prevent those tiny bubbles from escaping and is usually never more than half filled. Also preferable for any sparkling liquid, including ciders.

Cocktail or martini glass: Perfect for martinis and manhattans, remember that the stem is not just for show; it keeps hands from warming the drink. Available in three to six oz. sizes.

Coolers: These large-capacity tumblers are taller and hold a lot of ice for larger concoctions. They have become popular as of late for nonalcoholic and extra volume highballs.

Highball glass: Extremely versatile glass available in many sizes and used for almost any drink. Usually clear and tall, the most popular sizes range from 8 to 12 oz.

Hurricane glass: Tropical fruit drinks and bloody Marys are perfectly suited for these 16 to 23 oz. tall, curved glasses.

Rocks glasses: These "old fashioned" glasses hold from 6 to 10 oz. and are used for on-the-rocks presentations. Double rocks will run between 12 and 15 oz.

Shot glass: The old standby can also be used as a measuring glass and is a must for every bar.

MIXING TERMS

Build: In a glass full of ice, first pour in the liquor or spirit, then add the mixer. Add stirring/sizzle stick to stir the cocktail.

Fill: After you add ice and liquor or spirits, fill with mixer to within ¼ inch of the top.

Floating: To layer one ingredient on the top of a shot or cocktail.

Layering: Topping one ingredient over another.

Lychee (garnish): A tropical fruit tree native to Southern China, Indonesia, and east to the Philippines. Can be found in gourmet stores.

TYPES OF DRINKS

Aperitif: A light alcohol drink served before lunch or dinner, sometimes bitter.

Blended drinks: Blender drinks consisting of ice, ice cream and a variety of other ingredients blended until smooth though thick consistency.

Cobbler: A tall drink usually filled with crushed ice and garnished with fruit or mint.

Cream: Any drink made with ice cream, heavy cream, half-and-half or any of the famous bottled cream drinks.

Crusta: Served in a wine glass with sugar-coated rim and the inside of the glass lined with a citrus rind.

Cups: A traditionally British category of wine based drinks.

Daisy: An oversized cocktail sweetened with fruit syrup served over crushed ice.

Eggnog: A blend of milk or cream, beaten eggs, sugar, and liquor, usually rum, brandy, or whiskey and sometimes sherry topped with nutmeg.

Flip: Cold, creamy drinks made with eggs, sugar, alcohol, and citrus juice.

Highball: A tall drink usually served with whiskey and ginger ale. The favorite of many drinkers' grandparents.

Grog: A rum-based drink made with fruit and sugar.

Julep: A tall, sweet drink usually made with bourbon, water, sugar, crushed ice, and occasionally mint. The most popular julep being, of course, the Kentucky Derby's famous mint julep.

Mist: Any type of alcoholic beverage served over crushed ice.

Mojito: A Cuban-born drink prepared with sugar, muddled mint leaves, fresh lime juice, rum, ice, soda water, and garnished with mint leaves.

Puff: Made with equal parts alcohol and milk topped with club soda.

Pousse-café: A drink made with layers created by floating liqueur according to their density.

Rickey: A cocktail made of alcohol (usually whiskey, lime juice, and soda water).

Shooter: A straight shot of alcohol, also sometimes called serving a drink "neat."

Sling: A tall drink made with lemon juice and sugar and topped with club soda.

Sours: Drinks made with lemon juice, sugar, and alcohol.

Stixx: Tall, muddled cocktails using different-sized muddlers from six inches to twelve inches. Now they are muddling herbs, fruits, spices, and a variety of ethnic and regional ingredients including beans, roots, and spices.

Toddy: Served hot, it's a mixture of alcohol, spices, and hot water.

Toppers: Blended drinks with ice cream or crushed ice, the thicker the better, which is why these drinks are served with a spoon and a straw. They are made using cordials, flavored rums, flavored vodkas, blended fresh fruits, and tropical juices. They are topped with crushed candy, fruits, nuts, and just about anything you can eat with a spoon.

HOW TO RIM YOUR GLASS

Coating the rim of a glass with salt, sugar, or any other like substance adds a decorative touch that improves the presentation of the cocktail.

Simple steps:

Moisten the rim of the glass (ie., use a lime wedge to moisten the rim for a margarita).

Dip the rim in whatever ingredient you want to coat the glass with.

Slowly turn the glass to ensure you coat evenly.

Shake off any excess

Fill the glass with your prepared cocktail.

For more information and different cocktail rimmers, go to www.stirrings.com.

INDEX

Absolution, 8
Absolut squeeze, 9
Absolut vanilla vodka, 197
Absolut vodka, 6, 17, 35, 47, 50, 62, 106, 114, 185, 186, 187, 200, 207, 225,
    226, 230, 231, 246, 248
Absolut White Russian, 9
Adios, 10
Adios mother, 10
Affair, 10
Afterburner, 11
Agent O., 11
Air gunner, 11
Alabama slammer, 12
Alaskan iced tea, 12
Alexander the Great, 12
Alice-Be-Bananaless, 13
Allmonade, 13
Amber martini, 13
Ana's banana, 14
An Angel's kiss, 14
Anti-freeze, 14
Apple blossom, 14
Apple cider martini, 15
Apple Island iced tea, 15
Apple joll-e rancher, 15
Appletini, 15
Apricot cocktail, 16
Aqueduct, 16
Asian martini, 16
Atomic body slam, 16
Atomic waste, 17

B

Baby daddy, 17
Baby face, 17

C

D

G

Iron butterfly, 115
Island tea, 116
Italian screwdriver, 116

J

Jackie-o martini, 116
Jean-Marc XO vodka, 247
Jericho's breeze, 116
Jewel of Russia vodka, the, 248
Julius, 117
Jungle gardenia, 117
Jupiter juice, 117

K

Kamikaze, 117
Kamikaze shot, 118
Katt's meow classic, 118
Kaytusha rocket, 118
KBG, 119
Ketel One vodka, 247
Kiss (Kremlyovskaya is so sweet), 119
Knockout punch, 119
Kissable, 119
Kool-aid, 120
Krem de la krem, 120
Kremin glacier martini, 120
Kremlin colonel, 120
Kremlyovskaya chocolate vodka, 31, 45, 66, 119, 120, 121, 123, 189, 193
Kremlyovskaya raspberry rumble, 121
Kremlyovskaya vodka, 120, 172, 194, 206
Kretchma, 121
Kurant affair, 121
Kurant and 7 up, 122
Kurant juice break, 122

P

R

Russian knight, 172
Russian monk, 172

S

U

V

W

ABOUT THE AUTHOR

Ray Foley, a former Marine with over thirty years of bartending and restaurant experience, is Founder and Publisher of *Bartender Magazine*. *Bartender Magazine* is the only magazine in the world specifically geared towards bartenders and is one of the very few primarily designed for servers of alcohol. *Bartender Magazine* is enjoying its twenty-ninth year. It currently has a circulation of over 148,000 and is steadily growing.

After serving in the United States Marine Corps and attending Seton Hall University, Ray entered the restaurant business as a bartender, which eventually led to his position as Assistant General Manager of The Manor in West Orange, New Jersey, where he managed over 350 employees.

In 1983, Ray left The Manor to devote his full efforts to *Bartender Magazine*. The circulation and exposure has grown from 7,000 to over 148,000 to date and has become the largest on-premise liquor magazine in the country.

Ray has been published in numerous articles throughout the country and has appeared on TV and radio shows.

He is also the founder of the "Bartender Hall of Fame," which honors the best bartenders throughout the United States not only for their abilities as mixologists, but for involvement in their communities as well.

In addition, Ray is the founder of "The Bartenders' Foundation" Incorporated. This nonprofit foundation has been set up to raise scholarship money for bartenders and their families. Scholarships awarded to bartenders can be used to either further their education or can go toward the education of their children.

Mr. Foley serves as a consultant to some of our nation's foremost distillers and importers. He is also responsible for naming and inventing new drinks for the liquor industry, including "The Fuzzy Navel" and "The Royal Stretch."

Ray has one of the largest collections of cocktail recipe books in the world, dating back to the 1800s. He is one of the foremost collectors of cocktail shakers, with 368 shakers in his collection.

Ray is the author of *The Ultimate Cocktail Book; The Ultimate Little Shooter Book; The Ultimate Little Martini Book; The Ultimate Little Blender Book; Advice from Anonymous; Spirits of Ireland; Jokes, Quotes and Bartoons; X-Rated Drinks; Bartending for Dummies;* and *How to Run a Bar for Dummies.*

Ray resides in New Jersey with his wife and partner of twenty-five years, Jackie, and their son, Ryan. He is also the father of three other wonderful and bright children: Raymond Pindar, William, and Amy.

Ray is foremost, and always will be, a bartender.

For more information, please contact Jackie Foley at *Bartender Magazine,* PO Box 158, Liberty Corner, NJ 07938. Telephone: (908) 766-6006; FAX: (908) 766-6607; email: barmag@aol.com; website: www.bartender.com.